Cynthia K. Johnson
www.drcynthiajohnson.com
Printed in the United States of America
Amazon ISBN: 9798392938049

Stay in the know with upcoming books by signing up for my email list. I send out a new inspirational, devotional email once a month. Sign up at www.drcynthiajohnson.com.

"If anyone is thirsty, let him come to Me and drink. He who believes in Me, as the Scripture said, 'From his innermost being will flow rivers of living water.' But this He spoke of the Spirit, whom those who believed in Him were to receive."
John 7:37-39

TABLE OF CONTENTS

1 TO KNOW HIM AND ENJOY HIM

"Let not a wise man boast of his wisdom, and let not the mighty man boast of his might, let not a rich man boast of his riches; but let him who boasts boast of this, that he understands and knows Me" (Jeremiah 9:23-24).

MY HUSBAND AND I DROVE FOR MILES in the desert toward Grand Canyon National Park. We had friends who showed us pictures and spoke on and on about the spectacular sight. In the end, they could not express the experience to their satisfaction. All they could say was, "You have to experience it for yourself."

So, even though we had heard other people's stories and seen their pictures, we had no idea what we were about to encounter personally.

We drove around the top rim of the canyon to the first stop. The view was not immediately visible, so we parked at the viewpoint and walked around the display map.

As we came around the corner, we gasped in awe. Other tourists also gasped, in so much as we heard a great many "ooohs and aaaaahhs!"

Layers of God's creation unfolded before us. The air was electric. We were all stunned by the majesty and glory. The immense beauty was nothing that could be captured by a camera.

Our friends were right, we had to experience this for ourselves.

Similarly, dear reader, I want to help you learn how to encounter God's presence for yourself in greater glory than ever before. Throughout this book, I will take you through exercises step by step to help you learn how to experience your Creator God's presence to a greater degree, or maybe in a different way, than you have ever experienced Him.

Our Primary and Secondary Purpose

"For the Lord takes pleasure in His people" (Ps 149).

Our Primary Purpose

Most of us search our entire lives to understand the purpose for which we were born. We innately long to know that our life matters to the world around us. This is not a new phenomenon; humanity has searched for significance since sin destroyed the ideals for human life in the Garden of Eden.

Bible scholars, theologians, and Bible readers like you and me have studied this very thing in the Bible for centuries. One such study summarized their findings in a set of questions and answers in what is called, The Westminster Shorter Catechism. The very first question asks, "What is the chief end of man?" The answer states, "Man's chief end is to glorify God and to enjoy Him forever.[1]"

Think about that for a moment. God is God. He was not required to create you, but He chose to create you to enjoy friendship with you. He

---

[1] Westminster Shorter Catechism, http://www.ccel.org/ccel/anonymous/westminster1.i.i.html (30 Jun 2022) Also, Isa 43:7; Ps 16:11; John 17:22, 24; Matt 5:16; Deut 6:5; Mat 22:37; 1 Pet 2:9.

loves and values you! What He desires most is for you to choose to love Him in return!

The prophet Isaiah writes that we were made by God's love and for God's glory.[2] Moses taught the Israelites, "You shall love the Lord your God with all your heart and with all your soul and with all your might" (Deut 6:5). And Jesus calls this the greatest commandment of all.[3]

To love God is to enjoy Him because in His presence is fullness and joy.[4] So, our primary purpose on earth is this special love relationship with Him—**to love Him completely and enjoy His presence of love**.

God is love, and in His presence, we learn how to love. In His presence, He heals all our deepest wounds and fears. In His love we experience the fullness of life we were intended to have in the beginning in the Garden of Eden. In His presence, His love conforms us to the image of Christ. In His presence, His love teaches us how to walk in the Spirit. In this love relationship of knowing God intimately and fully, we find all we need for life.

Dear reader, when I learned this concept, my life became a lot simpler and more peaceful. As this little truth rooted itself deep inside my soul and grew, I began to shed lies, fears, hurts, false responsibilities, religious overwhelm, and burnout. I stopped striving to live by religious rules and relaxed. I began to learn more about being a loved child of God, to sense His presence, and enjoy Him.

Our Secondary Purpose

As we continue to grow in our primary purpose—to love Him and enjoy His love—we begin to live out our secondary purpose. Our

---

[2] Isa 43:7.

[3] Matt 22:37.

[4] Ps 16:11.

secondary purpose as beloved, royal children of God is to function as God's family representatives on earth.

We are called to this deeply personal relationship with Him to carry out His desires on earth through our talents, gifts, callings, and jobs. When we invite Him to work in us and through our lives, He is glorified. When people see God in the way we live and the things we do, His glory is manifested on earth.

Many people will never know God unless they see Him through us. When they see the glorious love relationship between us and our Creator God, they are drawn into a closer relationship with Him.

To Enjoy God, We Must Know God

However, when we attempt to fulfill our main purpose in life—to love God and enjoy His love—we encounter a major obstacle.

To enjoy God, we must know God.

Even when we think we "know" God, we can only glimpse at his nature through our limited human perceptions. We may intellectually know some things about God from the Bible, but most of us have not learned to consistently experience His love often enough to say we enjoy Him.

The overarching purpose of this book is to help you discover a more intimate relationship with your Creator and know His presence more intimately.

I challenge you to practice the following exercises and prayers with expectation and excitement. You will discover more of God's presence in your life here and now. For "He rewards those who diligently seek him" (Heb 11:6).

Cultivate God's Presence: Reflecting on Purpose

1. Have you ever considered your primary purpose in terms of enjoying God? Does this idea resonate with you in some way?
2. How does it feel when you consider such a proposition?
3. What does it mean to you to enjoy God?
4. Ask God to help you recognize His love.
5. Invite Him to work in and through your life.

Friend, I pray you will be surrounded by God's immense loving embrace today! I pray your spirit is sparked with excitement to know more about your Beloved! I pray for grace and peace to flow into all areas of your life!

Multiple Layers of Knowing God

As tourists, my husband and I drove around the rim of the Grand Canyon. So, in polite conversation, we could say we know the Grand Canyon.

In fact, we do know the Grand Canyon's spectacular wonder as a tourist in a general way, because we observed the lookout points along the rim. And yet, we could have taken the opportunity to learn more about the Grand Canyon at deeper levels.

As spectacular as the Grand Canyon is for the drive-by tourist, we could have taken more time at the informational displays and books. We could have taken a guided tour with a park ranger. We could have explored the canyon in more depth by taking a helicopter, plane, horse, mule, or raft to the bottom of the canyon.

We could have hiked down into the canyon and camped in its depths. If we were so inclined, we could study the Grand Canyon in very specialized ways as the geologists who study the layered rock formations and stream erosion, or the botanists who study the plant and tree species, or even as the meteorologists, who study how the Grand Canyon influences the weather.

If we were more committed to learning about the Grand Canyon, we could live in the area, because its residents know the moods and seasons of the canyon in a special and different way. Each of these people knows the majesty of the Grand Canyon in a unique way.

If we use my story as an analogy, we can peek over the rim into the deep canyon of who God is to explore the general and more specific ways we can know Him.

It is impossible to explore all the possibilities. However, I want to share with you some of the ways I have come to know Him in hopes that you will explore even deeper than I have into the masterful depths of our

Creator God. There are unfathomable depths to knowing our God, yet it is up to us how far we want to explore.

Knowing God by General Revelation

Just as there are different levels of knowing the Grand Canyon, there are also different levels and layers of knowing our Creator God.

When we stepped beyond the display map and turned the corner to see the Grand Canyon, the majesty of God was evident for all to see. We were caught up in the beauty of God through nature. Many people experience this kind of general revelation of God without realizing it. They are momentarily caught up in His peace and beauty through nature.[5] Many people feel closer to God in nature than anywhere else. This general revelation of God can be a stepping-stone to a deeper awareness and knowledge of God.

God has revealed Himself to all people in all places since the beginning of time through nature.[6] He desires that all people everywhere come to know Him, so He made all of creation to lead us to Himself! He wants to reveal Himself to us!

Revelation simply means an uncovering or unveiling.[7] In revelation God "unveils" Himself to us. He "discloses" and "uncovers" more about Himself to his creation.

God has revealed Himself to humanity through time, and He continues to reveal Himself to us today. He is God; He does not have to reveal Himself. However, the infinite God of the universe takes the initiative in making Himself known to us—His creation—His children.

---

[5] Rom 1:20.

[6] Acts 14:16; 17:26-27.

[7] Larry D. Hart, *Truth Aflame* (Grand Rapids, MI: Zondervan, 2005), 42.

What we know of God is only because He is gracious to share Himself with us. He desires to have fellowship with us; that's why we were created. From the beginning, He imparted His breath of life into humanity. It is His nature to impart the revelation of Himself. He wants to make Himself known. So even though our human nature is corrupted by sin, He continues to pursue a closer relationship with us!

If you are reading this, it is because He is drawing you to Himself, and you are curious. He loves that! He is concerned that His creatures know about Him and know Him intimately, even with the difficulties and boundaries constructed by sinful human nature! God takes the initiative in making Himself known and continues to reveal more and more of Himself **if we desire His company and are curious enough to seek Him.**[8]

The Problem with General Revelation

"An ox knows its owner, and a donkey its master's manger, but Israel does not know, My people do not understand" (Isa 1:3).

The problem is that general knowledge of God is not enough to bring humanity into an intimate relationship with Him. Adam and Eve's sin in Eden did not destroy God's general revelation. However, sin keeps us from coming to a more intimate knowledge of God. Our sinful nature distorts general revelation and tends to create our own distorted ideas of God—which is idolatry. God's people through the ages have continually denied the outstretched arms of their loving Father.

Even today, we continually turn away from Him—the One who longs to comfort and take care of us. Even when we say we love Him, we

---

[8] Jer 29:13

continually stray from His side. Sin of all kinds continues to tower between us and our Creator Father.

Knowing God by Special Revelation

However, God never leaves humanity without a way to know Him personally. So, into the vacuum of human sinfulness, God sends forth special revelation.[9] We can feel His presence and have a personal experience with Him because revelation is personal. **God wants us to know and love Him.**[10]

God reveals Himself to humanity in personal ways. He is always near even when we are unaware. By His nature, He is everywhere present (omnipresent). Yet, God's presence is manifest (revealed) to us when we become aware of and recognize Him.

In Old Testament times, God revealed Himself in special revelation to the patriarchs and prophets and then in the New Testament through His Son, Jesus Christ!

Many people experience a taste of God's manifest presence in a serene moment in nature or a church worship service. Yet, for most Christians, the idea of a deep and continual practice of the presence of God is a foreign concept.

We will explore knowing God's presence in special revelation more thoroughly. You will develop the awareness and sensitivity to experience His manifest presence at all times. The following exercises will take your relationship with our Creator Father, Savior, and Friend to a deeper and more satisfying level. You will come to know God more intimately than ever before! Let's look at a few foundational concepts for knowing God.

---

[9] Heb 1:1-2.

[10] Millard J. Erickson, *Christian Theology* (Grand Rapids, MI: Baker Academic, 2005), 202.

Biblically, What Does It Mean to Know God?

The Hebrew Word *"Yada"*

So, what does it mean to "know" God and His presence? In the English language, when we say we "know" something, it generally means we have some level of intellectual information about a subject—like I thought I knew the Grand Canyon.

However, the most common word translated as "know" or "knowledge" in the Old Testament comes from the root word, *yada*. *Yada* appears almost 950 times in the Hebrew Bible and has a broader meaning than the English word "know." This "knowing" indicates a type of intimacy, as in Genesis 4:1 where, "Adam *knew* Eve his wife, and she conceived."

Adam and Eve knew their Creator God in the most intimate relationship possible, Spirit to spirit, Creator to creation. He was the Center of their existence. They could perceive Him with their senses and in their inner being. At the very thought of their Father, they had a sense of His presence.

Adam and Eve knew God intimately as a true reality that permeated their lives completely in every possible way. Every day they dwelt in His peace, love, joy, security, fulfillment, and abundance of provision. The intimate knowledge of God they experienced is hard for us to even imagine today with the effects of sin in our nature. But we continue to learn and grow into all the fullness of life Jesus came to bring.

The Biblical Context of "Know"

Additionally, in the Biblical Hebrew context, to "know" means not only to be intellectually informed but to apprehend and experience; it is the exercise or actualization of information. It means to perceive (as revelation), to learn in various ways, to understand, to will, to perform, and to experience.[11]

So, the Hebrew definition of "know" means more than simply a good idea or a concept. Knowing a thing means it becomes incorporated into one's heart and lifestyle.

Just because we heard something one time does not mean we "know" it completely or live as though the idea influences our daily life. It is possible to know something intellectually, and yet not experience the fullness of its meaning. It might take a long time to know a concept so deeply, that it becomes incorporated into who we are as a person.

For example, many of us know in our minds we should eat healthier, but it takes a while for us to incorporate the healthier things we know into our daily routines. We take our time learning about healthier foods and new habits. Our relationship with food can be complicated at times, and we are reluctant to change old habits. Yet, to maintain a healthier lifestyle, we must cultivate the relationship between our knowledge and our actions.

Likewise, as we learn to experience God's amazing presence, we build a relationship between our knowledge and actions as well.

So, you see in the Bible, knowing God is not simply obtaining intellectual knowledge, but also developing a relationship with heart knowledge that continues to grow until our knowledge is lived as a lifestyle every day with ongoing interactions.

---

[11] G. Kittel, G. W. Bromiley and G. Friedrich, ed., "γινώσκω, γνῶσις, ἐπιγινώσκω, ἐπίγνωσις," *Theological Dictionary of the New Testament* (Grand Rapids, MI: Eerdmans, 1964),1:698; Carl Schultz, "know, knowledge," *Baker Theological Dictionary of the Bible*, ed. Walter A. Elwell (Grand Rapids, MI: Baker Books, 2000), 457-458.

Ongoing Interactions

My daughter had a baby a few years ago. When I arrived and met baby Abigail, I didn't know much about her. I knew her name and her parents. I knew some general things about babies and the ways babies might respond. But I didn't know Abigail.

As I spent time with Abigail, I began to learn more about her. I learned how she liked to be held, what kind of bounce she preferred, and how she would not take a pacifier. But I still didn't know all there is to know about her. As time passed, I continued to learn more about her and spend more time with her.

As a toddler, we experienced a different kind of relationship than when she was a newborn. And now that she is an 8-year-old, we experience an even different type of relationship. With her development physically, mentally, emotionally, socially, and spiritually, etc., our relationship continues to grow in different ways with different experiences and new wonders.

Likewise, we continue to know God through our continued experiences with Him. As we grow mentally, emotionally, and spiritually, our relationship with God continues with new wonder. We have new experiences together. Just as Abby and I went from playing peekaboo to blocks to Barbies to video games, we as children of God also grow in our experiences with our Lord. Knowing God is a continual process of discovery and delight, of communing and conversing with Him in ongoing interactions.

We can know general things about God, but we can only know Him truly by relationship experience with Him. Of course, we learn much about God from the Bible. And if all you want to know is the Bible, you must simply study hard and learn from teachers who know the Bible.

However, if you want to know the God of the Bible intimately, you must have ongoing personal interactions with Him. You must talk to

Him, ask Him questions, consult Him in day-to-day life situations, and listen. There is no other way.

In the Christian classic book, *Practicing His Presence*, Brother Lawrence came to form the habit of conversing with God in ongoing interactions continually. Lawrence came to know God so profoundly that his times of worship and prayer were no different than other times of the day. He exhorts,

> Let me put it this way: before we can love, we must know. We must know someone before we can love him. How shall we keep our "first love" for the Lord? By constantly knowing Him better! Then how shall we know the Lord? We must often turn to Him, think of Him, behold Him. Then our hearts will be found with our treasure.[12]

When we turn often toward God and think of Him and behold His goodness, our love grows larger and larger. Paul instructs believers not to "set" their minds on earthy, fleshly things but on things that are above, heavenly, Godly things.[13] We can turn our hearts and minds to think about Him and ponder His nature and ways. We turn those thoughts into communication, and thus we have ongoing interactions with Him throughout our day.

In this manner, we continue to learn more about Him and learn to love Him more intimately. No matter how much we think we know about God already, we have not scratched the surface of coming to know Him in the depth He desires.

When I first saw baby Abigail, I knew the love of a grandparent. But when she smiled and grasped my finger, I loved her more, then as she grew and gave me a great big toddler hug, ohh, my, how my heart leapt.

---

[12] Brother Lawrence and Frank Laubach, ed. Gene Edwards, *Practicing His Presence* (Jacksonville, FL: The SeedSowers), 45, 85.

[13] Rom 8:5; Col 3:2.

Now, when I spend the night, we read, snuggle, and have the most wonderful conversations! We keep growing and learning new things about each other. The only way I continue to know my granddaughter is to have ongoing interactions with her, and we are still learning and growing in our relationship together.

Similarly, we grow in love with our Lord. He woos us and draws us to Himself at the beginning of our relationship with Him. He wraps us in His love and peace, and we experience His love inside and out. We continue to experience new levels of growth and development in our relationship with each interaction. We grow from glory to glory as we experience more of His presence in ongoing interactions with Him.

Cultivate God's Presence: Knowing God in Revelation

1. Think about moments you have experienced the general revelation of God in nature. Do you feel closer to God in nature?
2. Thank God for His special revelations given to us in Jesus Christ. Ask Him to reveal more of Himself to you.
3. What is one thing you would ask Jesus if He were sitting beside you chatting like your best friend?

2 AWAKENING TO GOD'S PRESENCE

"With loving-kindness have I drawn thee" (Jer 31:3).

EVERY BELIEVER IS ON A JOURNEY OF growing in their love relationship with God. Let me assure you that growing in your relationship is not unattainable. We have the capacity to know and love Him deeply because we are His children, made in His image. In this chapter, we will focus on the process of awakening to more of God's presence.

My Story Toward a Deeper Awareness

I was born to Christian parents, and I don't remember the moment I first gave my heart to Christ. So, I have been at this Christian thing for a long time.[14]

Yet, it was not until I was in my thirties that I awoke to a deeper experience of God's dynamic presence.

I had dedicated some time each morning to prayer, Scriptures, and an exercise I will share with you, when I began to experience an internal kind of goose-bumpy feeling—not the *fear* kind of goose-bumpy feeling. It was immense *peace* and *love*.

---

[14] Some information in this section is taken from, C.K. Johnson, *The 90-Day Spiritual Awakening Journal: Simple Exercises to Discover God's Presence in Everyday Life* (Spokane, WA: Deeper Walk Ministries, 2019).

I would describe it, as Revivalist Charles Finney did long ago, as "liquid love." I already knew God in many ways. I knew Him in salvation and baptism. I knew Him in heart-stirring praise and worship. I knew Him in the gifts I experienced, and in prayers of all kinds. And I had also been to glorious revival meetings where I had encountered God in miraculous ways.

These were all precious moments, but not sustained daily experiences.

I had heard people talk about "abiding in Christ" and "practicing the presence" of God, but I did not understand what they meant. However, with this new experience of "liquid love" being stirred in my heart, I was awakened to more of His presence.

What Does God's Presence Feel Like?

God's presence can be felt in various ways. It can feel like an internal kind of goose-bumpy feeling liquid love kind of feeling. Sometimes it can feel like a prod in the right direction you know is right.

God's presence can feel like lightness or joy in your heart. It can feel like a deep sense of "knowing" something. It can feel like strength to face difficulty, or it can feel like peace that envelopes you.

God's presence is always peace, love, and joy—never anxiety, fear, or hate. The Bible promises that our Creator Father will send us the "Comforter."[15] So, His presence feels like the safety and comfort of home. He is our Creator, and His presence is our origin—where we belong.

---

[15] John 14:16 KJV.

Awakening to More

"Awake, sleeper, and arise from the dead, and Christ will shine on you" (Ephesians 5:14).

Many people live their entire lives unaware of God's glorious presence. Perhaps some people will turn toward Him occasionally, yet most people have little, if any, awareness of His presence in day-to-day life. It is as if people go through life without being truly awake spiritually.

It is easy (even for Christians) to go through life and not wonder about their relationship with their Creator Father, or the meaning of life and spiritual things. Most people spend years growing and learning how to function in the physical world and yet have not recognized the need to develop their personal spirits. It is as if they are spiritually asleep.

From the beginning, we were created children of our Father, the God of all spirits, as human spirit, soul, and body. We spend all our lives growing physically, mentally, and emotionally, yet we neglect to grow spiritually in our inner being. Many of us are unaware of our personal spirit. We are spiritually asleep.

Just as our bodies sleep through the night and the outside world continues, the spiritual world also continues, even if we are unaware of it. God is Spirit and surrounds us each moment like the air we breathe. We have opportunities to connect with Him throughout our day and night whether we are aware enough to recognize it or not. So how do you know if you are asleep or awake to God's presence? Below are some indicators.

Asleep Indicators

Because we are human, we all have areas where we are spiritually asleep and areas where we are spiritually awake. This journey of faith consists of many different moments where we encounter God in ways that awaken our spirits to more of Him and the spiritual world around us. We all tend to slip in and out of cycles of sleepiness and alertness.[16]

However, believers whose personal spirits are slumbering may know God is present in corporate worship by faith, but do not experience His love in an intensely personal way.

In prayer, they are unable to sustain continuing communication because prayer feels dry and dull and their mind wanders. They will say, "I believe God is aware of our worship, but I have never experienced what you are talking about."

Personal Scripture reading for the less awake person becomes cognitive reading or study without the quickening breath of God speaking through the Scriptures. Such persons may feel a flicker of God's presence for a moment but are unable to stay and rest in His presence and are distracted by many things. Their personal spirit is not awake enough to experience the reality of God's continuing and abiding presence.

Awake Indicators

Believers with an awakened personal spirit feel Him moving inside. God quickens their personal spirits and enables spiritual worship in a more deeply, stirring way.[17]

In times of private prayer and devotion, the person with a more awakened personal spirit can read Scripture, pray, and worship with a real sense of refreshing, strengthening, and love in Jesus Christ's presence.

They can enjoy a quiet devotional time because their personal spirit can soar, unimpeded by the demands and distractions of other people.

---

[16] John Loren Sandford and Paula Sandford, *Awakening the Slumbering Spirit* (Lake Mary, FL: Charisma House, 2008), 62.

[17] John 4:23-24.

Their senses are heightened by being surrounded by His love. True worship in Spirit becomes a reality.

This environment can be a rewarding time of worship and intimacy with the Lord. Believers who have awakened personal spirits grow toward more security in their inner person and learn to relax and focus on time spent alone with God. They learn to entertain His presence as they commune daily with the Spirit of God.

Each person possesses an individualized spiritual and emotional temperament. There are obviously different personality types, yet even the extrovert can enjoy the awareness of God's presence in this kind of silence. We were all created to enjoy the refreshing rest and peace of God's manifest presence.

Spiritual Awareness and Response

"Every one of us is as close to God as he has chosen to be."
—J. Oswald Sanders

Many of us have spent years striving to serve God, including me. In my growth process, I have come to learn that God does not merely want His people to believe in Him, memorize verses, recite prayers, or work for Him. Although those things are important and good, sometimes we can mindlessly go through the motions and not know how to connect our hearts with His heart. Mindless motions and mental knowledge alone leave our hearts unsatisfied and unfulfilled.

God wants us to know Him in our minds and hearts. He wants to converse and interact with us—His children—intimately and personally in ongoing interactions. Through this intimate connection, God wants to reveal Himself to us in deeper and more profound dimensions.

Thus, we must continually cultivate awareness and response to respond to the Lord's intimate and gentle knocking.

The Stirring of Awareness

In the Garden of Eden, humans existed in unhindered intimacy until sin created barriers to our awareness of Him. Through Christ's work on the cross, we can enter that deep awareness and intimacy with our Creator God once again. However, now we must work through all the sinful obstacles that would hinder our search for a deeper relationship.

Along the journey, there are times when we sense a deep and indisputable stirring in our human spirit. Most of us do not know what to do with our unsettled feelings. The hunger or agitation can be bewildering and confusing. These inner longings or stirrings are so real, they cannot be ignored. The unrest or uneasiness we feel is simply our human spirit's response to God's drawing. The magnetic attraction of God's nearness pulls us toward Him, and the result is dissatisfaction with the status quo. Yet, many people misunderstand.

Some people are excited, and some are confused. Many people are misguided and attempt to satisfy their spiritual hunger with physical things. Others misunderstand God's drawing power as a craving of the body or soul and may fill the void with good works or material things.

For example, when Moses was a young man, God awakened Moses' personal spirit to draw him closer to Himself, yet Moses mistook God's stirring for the pursuit of social action in the flesh.[18] However, after spending time with God in his wilderness season, Moses' plan was deconstructed to make room for God's plan.

When Moses learned how to respond to the stirring call of God's presence in his life, then he was able to secure freedom for Israel in God's time and in God's way. First and foremost, we are all called to an intimate relationship with our Creator Father as His children before He can trust us with additional areas of rulership in His kingdom.

---

[18] Exod 2:11-13.

The Gift of Response

In the Scriptures, we read about saints who responded to the stirring for more of God and how they came to know Him intimately during their lifetimes.

These men and women came to know God in extraordinary ways. For example, Enoch was so close to God that God simply took him. He existed one day and disappeared into the heavenly realm the next day without seeing death.

Moses grew to experience an amazing relationship with God. He witnessed God's incredible power in public miracles and private face-to-face conversations.

Abraham was called the friend of God and the Father of the Faith. David was called a man after God's own heart. These and many other people of faith like them cultivated an intensely intimate and personal relationship with God.

When I began pondering the Fathers and Mothers of our Faith, I wondered what these ancients had in common that sparked their deep relationships with God. Since God does not show favoritism, I wondered what was the key to their intimate relationship with God? Then I came across A.W. Tozer's suggestion,

> The one vital quality which they [the saints of old] had in common was spiritual receptivity. Something in them was open to heaven, something which urged them Godward. Without attempting anything like a profound analysis, I shall say simply that they had spiritual awareness, and that they went on to cultivate it until it became the biggest thing in their lives. They differed from the average person in that when they felt the inward longing they *did something about it* [Tozer's emphasis]. They acquired the lifelong habit of spiritual response.[19]

---

[19] A.W. Tozer, *The Pursuit of God*, (Camp Hill, Pennsylvania: Christian

The saints of old cultivated awareness, receptivity, and response.

Awareness is a gift of God's grace to be sure, but it must be recognized and cultivated as any other gift. I know many people who are incredibly gifted but have never pursued those gifts. You, too, probably know someone who has underrealized gifts, talents, and abilities.

Sports broadcasters in the United States talk about how American football star, Tom Brady, performed better at 45 years of age than he did at 25. He is commonly called the GOAT (Greatest of All Time), because he has worked and refined his skills through the years. Of course, he began with a God-given gift for sports, but He has cultivated his gift.

The same principle holds true in our spiritual lives. The ancient Fathers and Mothers of Bible times cultivated their relationship skills with their Creator. They learned to recognize God's presence and made a habit of responding. They developed the lifelong habit of awareness and response. Even today every person can learn to cultivate this same Spiritual awareness and response.

"Open my eyes, that I may see wondrous things from Your law"
Psalm 119:18 (NKJV).

Breakthrough Moments

To grow in awareness of God's intimate presence, we need a break in our usual way of thinking and perceiving. This is a transitional breakthrough moment where we get a glimpse into deeper dimensions of reality.

This breakthrough moment could happen in a time of crisis, a time of pressing in to seek the Lord, or a time of questioning life. Sometimes, this breakthrough moment comes as we get honest with ourselves and

Publications, Inc., 1993), 63.

God in a quiet moment. This mysterious moment becomes a catalyst experience where we open the door wider to God and life in His Spirit. We become more awake.

People long to awaken to this mysterious spiritual depth, but most people need help to discover its elusiveness, because many people are simply stuck, or maybe they are locked in a way of thinking that denies anything unexplainable by logical or scientific means. There must be an openness in our hearts that allows for the possibility of spiritual experiences. We must learn to acknowledge the spiritual, as well as the natural.

The point is that we can facilitate breakthrough moments. This is the whole purpose of the accompanying exercises in this book. The exercises help you set your mind on God.[20] They help you learn how to recognize His presence and respond to His loving embrace. They help you learn spiritual skills for seeking God every day, right where you are. For we know He rewards those who diligently seek Him.

---

[20] Col 3:2.

Cultivate God's Presence: Awakening to Know God More Intimately

We must exercise our human spirit to grow in awareness of the Kingdom of God. Here are a few simple ideas and exercises to help you get started in cultivating more awareness of His presence. We will add to these and go into more depth as we go along.

So, because information and revelation are not enough for transformation, stop and do one of these exercises right now.

1. **Believe.** Keep an open and expecting heart (Heb 3:12). You may have to repent for a negative attitude or an unbelieving heart. Decide in your heart and declare with your mouth you are going to be open to spiritual wonder.

2. **Bible meditation.** Practice thinking about a Bible verse. Maybe write a verse on an index card and put it on your bathroom mirror, or any place you will see it throughout the day. Suggestion: "I am the vine, you are the branches. He who abides in Me, and I in him, bears much fruit; for without Me you can do nothing" (John 15:5 NKJV).

3. **Bible App.** Listen to the Bible on a phone app. Listen to whole sections or books at a time. Whether you notice anything the first time or not, be certain the experience is washing your soul. You will notice a difference in your attitude and other things specific to

you after a few times. Suggestion: Listen to the book of Ephesians every day for a month.

4. **Car or chore time.** Use your time in the car or time doing routine chores to pray, listen to worship music, or the Bible.

5. **Pondering the cross.** Practice taking a few moments to think about the cross of Christ. Think about and picture His blood being shed for you. This is very powerful. Many people report experiences with Jesus, and some people have experienced healing in this way.

6. **Fasting.** Practice occasional fasting (Isa 58). Research this if you have never fasted before.

7. **Sharing.** Share your experiences with a trusted friend, who is also pursuing intimacy with God. Sometimes you gain awareness, discernment, and perspective as you share with one another.

If you are being blessed in any way, please share your thoughts on Amazon.com by leaving a review for How to Practice the Presence of God. Your experiences and insights provide valuable information for other potential readers. I truly appreciate your help in sharing the message of God's loving presence with others! Thank you so very much!

The Best Attitude

"Who then is greatest in the Kingdom of heaven?' And He called a child to Himself and set him before them, and said, 'Truly I say to you, unless you are converted and become like children, you will not enter the Kingdom of heaven. Whoever then humbles himself as this child, he is the greatest in the Kingdom of heaven'" (Matthew 18:1-4).

One day, another of my granddaughters got mad. The tiny 3-year-old stomped out the door and began down our 100-yard gravel driveway. The problem was she was barefooted. She took a few steps flat-footed, then walked on the side of her foot, then on her toes. Her face was red and determined.

She swung her hair from side to side and tried to push through. We let her go until she got tired of doing things her way. Then my husband in his sturdy work boots swooped her up in his strong arms to save her from herself. He brought her in, loved on her, and gave her a popsicle. She soon realized she was completely dependent on us for survival.

Likewise, we can be headstrong children sometimes and must recognize our complete dependence on God and His goodness to us. When we begin to realize the depths of sin in our stubborn human nature, and that we are in absolute poverty of spirit without Jesus' saving grace, then we begin to experience a child-like dependence on the true Source of Life.

In the above verse, the disciples argued among themselves as to who was the greatest. At first, they did not understand the Kingdom of God was a spiritual kingdom, because they were fighting about earthly power, status, and position. Jesus confronted their pride by declaring that they must be converted and humble themselves like a little child.

Jesus replied, "Unless *you change*, . . . you will never enter the kingdom." In a blow to the disciples' ego, Jesus set a little child before them, and indicated the child was greater than they.

Why would Jesus say such a thing? I venture to guess there are several reasons, and maybe the following are part of the answer.

Dependency and Trust. Little children are dependent. Little children are helpless and dependent on their parents for everything. They depend on adults for protection and provision. Even determined ones recognize their need for dependence, which brings a humble attitude of trust. When we arrive at the attitude that breathes, "I cannot even begin to do this without You, Lord," then Jesus says that we are indeed blessed and esteemed in the Kingdom of heaven. It is then that His grace becomes more powerful than our need, for He gives His empowering grace to the humble.[21]

Humility. Speaking generally, a small child is humble for the most part and not concerned about status. They continually ask questions because they are constantly reminded that they do not know how to live in this world. When we begin to think we have things all figured out, we develop a proud spirit. Little children take direction and correction in humility as they try to make sense of their world.

A Curious and Teachable Spirit. Little children are teachable. Adults are always correcting little children's words and actions. Most little children know they do not understand fully and are willing to learn.

They are curious about everything. So, little children ask infinite "why" questions. They may even have trouble shutting their curiosity down enough to sleep at night. For them, the world is full of exciting possibilities.

---

[21] 1 Peter 5:5.

Awakening Our Curiosity

As adults, somewhere along the path, life shuts down our curiosity, and we lose the thrill of discovery. We lose the nudge of curiosity that speaks wonder to our hearts.

Curiosity establishes a deep interest in the things of life and the things of God. All these things are important to God. We must establish that insatiable curiosity again. We must begin to ask questions. We must begin to notice how beautiful the world is and decide to see its beauty. We must cultivate a life full of curiosity, wonder, and awe.

The Holy Spirit will teach, guide, and direct; however, many times as humans we tend to lean on our understanding and forget to ask questions. James writes bluntly, "You do not have because you do not ask" (Jas 4:2). Jesus teaches, "Ask, and it will be given to you" (Matt 7:7 NKJV). To ask questions means we are cultivating a childlike faith, curiosity, and trust.[22] It means we are keeping our hearts open, aware, and dependent on our Creator Father.

Asking questions is the best way to know what the Lord thinks of a thing or situation. Certainly, His thoughts will be higher, more loving, and more strategic than our thoughts. His answers will be truth.

At times adults have hindered a child's spirit by responding with an arrogant attitude to a child's question so that the child began to believe questions were wrong, dumb, or foolish. For whatever reason, many of us somewhere in the process of maturity have stopped asking questions.

The Lord loves to teach His children. He wants to be our Father. He wants to heal our emotional father wounds and show us His nature in perfect Fatherly love. He desires for us to embrace our nature as His children.

---

[22] Mark 10:15.

This is the kind of ideal relationship He had with Adam and Eve in the Garden of Eden. He loves His children to inquire of Him, and He loves leading His children on the exciting adventure of discovery.

Through this kind of intimate interaction, we begin to learn His ways, and He heals our trauma and dispels the lies we believe about Him. We learn to turn to Him continually in daily life in ongoing interactions to ask for His opinion and insight. In the process of asking and learning, we begin to discover that the dynamic relationship with our Father becomes the most important part. In His presence we find healing, love, security, provision, purpose, peace, and rest. We find everything we need in His abiding love.

Cultivate God's Presence: Healing Prayer for Childhood Wounds

My Prayer for You: Dear Lord, I pray for readers today that you would heal the places inside their hearts where someone crushed their curiosity as a child. Send your precious Spirit to heal the sting of rejection, the pain of not being heard or understood, the unspeakable traumas.

I ask you to cover them in your blood and wrap their hearts in your amazing love to heal all that would hinder their curiosity. Awaken their spirits to your love. Awaken their childlike passion, curiosity, and wonder! Thank you for your healing peace that reaches deep in their souls. In Jesus' name, Amen.

Because we were born into this world of imperfect parents, we all have some sort of parental wounding.

Exercise Steps:

Step 1. Simply come to the Lord honestly as a little child and bring to Him all your hurt and disappointments. Imagine yourself putting it all into His hands. It is too heavy a load for you to continue to carry.

Step 2. Ask forgiveness for not understanding what it means to be God's child. Ask for His forgiveness for not coming to Him sooner (and anything else on your mind).

Step 3. Ask God to help you to forgive the authority figures in your life. Even if you do not feel you can forgive, by faith decide to forgive those who have squelched your curiosity as a child. Forgive those who caused you to grow up too fast. By faith, ask blessings for them.

Step 4. At this moment, ask Jesus to bring healing to your emotions and memories.

This may bring up uncomfortable and unhealed emotions. Praying this simple prayer will help many people. Others will need more time and prayer. Some will need guidance from a sensitive godly counselor or prayer minister. Don't be afraid to find whatever level of help you need to heal.

Read slowly and accept my prayer for you below. Allow time for the Holy Spirit to minister to your heart.

My Prayer For You, Dear Reader: I thank You, Jesus, for coming to die for all of our sins. I ask You to cover these ones in Your precious blood and forgive them. I ask You to give them the grace to forgive those who have hurt them severely. I ask for Your grace to strengthen and empower them now.

Lord, You are amazing! I ask you to heal this reader's heart right now. Take away the sting of pain as they pray today! Bring peace to his/her heart. I speak the undeniable peace of God to you now. Lord, I ask You to help this one be open and curious about Your intimate work. Thank you! Amen.

The Element of Desire

"You will seek me and find me when you search for Me with all your heart" (Jer 29:13).

The Scriptures exhort us repeatedly to humble ourselves and set our hearts to seek God with wholehearted desire.[23] We are exhorted to make God the greatest treasure in life and to love Him with all our heart, soul, mind, and strength. King David cautioned his son, Solomon, to serve God willingly **with his whole heart**, and then he said, "If you seek Him, He will let you find Him" (1 Chr 28:9).

Deeper intimacy with God requires intentional cultivation of spiritual awareness and response to God's gracious overtures. God longs for us to know Him and understand His ways. He promises that we will find Him when we seek Him completely from our hearts.[24]

Desire is a Spiritual Thermometer

A person's desire has everything to do with whether or not he or she draws close to God. It is the person, not God, who determines the level of desire. God always desires closeness with us. We humans are the ones that waver in desire.

The desire cycle runs like this: We can increase desire by exercise, or we can destroy desire by neglect. We increase desire by being aware of the thoughts we think and where we place our affections. The things we focus on grow larger in our hearts and minds. The things we do not focus on fade away.

For example, the more we eat junk food, the more junk food we want. The more we feed our minds on movies, the more movies we want to

---

[23] 1 Chr 22:19.; 2 Tim 1:6; 2 Pet 1:13; 2 Pet 3:1.

[24] Deut 4:29; Jer 29; Prov 3:5; Joel 2:12.; Hos 6:6; Jer 9:23-24.

watch. The more chocolate I eat, the more I want. Then if I make a habit of having chocolate at 2:30 every afternoon, well you know what happens. Our flesh wants what it wants, and the examples are endless.

However, our desire can fade with neglect. When we neglect our current favorite television show for several months, the desire fades. As another example, when we graduate college or high school and leave town for years, our desire to get together with most of the people we once saw daily fades too.

In our relationship with God, our level of desire for friendship with God can increase or fade as well. Our desire can be a spiritual thermometer that indicates where we are in our relationship. When fervent desire slides into passivity for God's presence and the things of God, we know we have lost our spiritual appetite and have become spiritually weak or ill.

Life gets difficult for us all sometimes, and it is easy to let other important things take priority. Yet, when we allow other things to gravitate to the center of our lives instead of God, we risk holding onto idols instead of God.

God understands our crazy lives. He just wants to walk through it with us.

Cultivate God's Presence: Increasing Desire

Because information and revelation alone are not enough for transformation, do one of these now before the moment fades.

1. **Acknowledge You Need Help.** When we acknowledge we are not enough and need help, a deep longing for God's intervention is created in our hearts. It is important to be honest about our tendency to wander from sincere devotion and dependence on Him. Forgive yourself and ask God to forgive you for wandering. Simply begin again. His mercies and grace are new each morning. He loves you and will draw you nearer than ever before!

2. **Memorize these verses.**
   a. Psalm 27:4
   b. Psalm 42:1-2
   c. Hebrews 11:6
   d. 1 Peter 2:2

3. **Connection to the Body of Christ.** Worship and pray with others who are full of passion and desire. In the spirit, it is like taking your little fading ember and joining together other hot coals until you ignite into a hot burning flame.

4. **Exercise Spiritually**. When we practice spiritual exercises (such as Bible reading, fasting, praying, and other practices like those in this book), we begin to focus more on Him, and our desire increases.

The Problem of Busyness

"The Lord looks down from heaven on all humankind to see if there are any who understand, any who seek God" (Psalms 14:2).

Life gets busy for all of us, and it can be hard to find time to think about God between, family, work, school, household chores, and trips to the grocery store. When our heart is occupied with many things, we are unlikely to seek the companionship of God's presence. If our heart becomes full of life's business, we may lose our fervent passion and become apathetic or unconcerned. We become too full of earthly activity to crave heavenly activity. Proverbs 27:7 describes it like this, "A satisfied person despises [tramples] honey, But to a hungry person any bitter thing is sweet."

A familiar picture will illustrate this point. All cultures have a time of feasting to celebrate a holiday. In the United States, we have several holidays throughout the year whose centerpiece is a huge feast. Many of us skip breakfast to increase our appetite for the holiday meal. We snack all morning, then when it is time to eat, we eat and eat, and groan because we ate too much. A couple of hours later we may go to another family member's house for another meal. The second meal may be greater and tastier, yet if we have already eaten, we are not hungry. We are full and may nibble or brush aside the food because we are not hungry.

A similar thing happens to church people and spiritual things. Many people do not despise God's presence, but compared to a hungry person, they may be casual or indifferent toward pursuing Him. Often temporal life things squeeze out time with God, and after a while, desire for God diminishes. For many people, passion for God becomes a distant memory.

Christians in the Middle Ages were concerned about the sin of sloth, which most of us have never heard about. The sin of sloth is a passive attitude that gives up seeking God wholeheartedly. Sloth is a sin that goes beyond disobedience and rebellion because it continues to look religious on the outside yet is stagnant on the inside.[25]

Revelation 3:16 warns believers about allowing material things to satisfy their souls, as did the "lukewarm" Laodicean church. The farther we drift from passionate devotion to Christ, the heavier we experience life's load. We diligently seek things to fill the void and help us cope with life. The closer we are to His strength, the greater our strength and the easier it is to handle life's situations.

A busy lifestyle squeezes out time with our Lord, and then interest in the Scriptures dwindles and desire for prayer fades. As a result, His presence and the life-giving flow of the Spirit recedes, and the Word does not come alive in our spirit as it could, or once did. We think of Him less frequently and hear His voice less and less. Life's problems begin to feel heavier and heavier.

Yet, when we decide to spend more time in His Word and prayer, He will meet us there. The deeper we go into His love, the easier it is for us to make time for Him. Our burdens become lighter because He refreshes us and gives us strength and strategies to overcome life's obstacles.

---

[25] Stephen Eyre, *Drawing Close to God* (Downers Grove, IL: InterVarsity Press, 1995), 18-19.

Cultivate God's Presence: Simple Habits Even When You Are Busy

"Set your mind on the things above, not on the things that are on earth" (Col 3:2).

I believe we can learn to maintain a heart of openness and sensitivity to God's presence even when our physical lives are busy. Here are five easy ideas to add small habits into a busy lifestyle that will increase your awareness, receptivity, and desire. Remember to ask for help and trust His goodness.

1. Find small times during your day to turn your heart to think exclusively about Jesus. You can think about a Scripture, Christian music, a picture of Him in your mind, a prayer phrase, the cross, the empty tomb, or something that helps focus your mind on Jesus. Use time in the car, time during routine chores, time in the shower, lunchtime, a few minutes with morning coffee, or a few minutes before bed.

2. Deliberately take five minutes out of a day, or one minute out of every sixty to think on Him. It is good to focus on something for which you are grateful.

3. Put a reminder in your phone app to remind you to set your mind on things above—on Jesus!

4. Put a rubber band on your wrist to remind you to stop for a minute and think about Him.

5. Make a habit to think your last thoughts before sleep and the first thoughts when waking about Christ.

My Prayer for You: Dear Lord, I ask that you draw readers close to you. Shine your revealing healing light on their situations. I ask you to enable and strengthen them to pursue you wholeheartedly. Stir their desire. Awaken their spiritual senses to receive all the glorious adventures in Your kingdom! Open their hearts to more of Your love. Strengthen their resolve and discipline to pursue You further! Amen!

~ ~ ~

Dear Reader,

I would be incredibly grateful if you could share your thoughts on Amazon by leaving a review for this book, How to Practice the Presence of God.

Reviews play a crucial role in helping others discover the book, and your insights can provide valuable information for readers.

To leave a review, you can search Amazon.com for How to Practice the Presence of God or go to the following address:
https://www.amazon.com/How-Practice-Presence-Step-Step/dp/B0C2SVRQHD/

Thank you again! If you have any questions or if there's anything else I can do for you, please don't hesitate to get in touch.

I truly appreciate your help in sharing the message of God's loving presence with others!

Cynthia Johnson

3 KNOWING CHRIST IN YOU

"He who believes in Me, as the Scripture said, 'From his innermost being will flow rivers of living water.'" But this He spoke of the Spirit, whom those who believed in Him were to receive" (John 7:37-39).

How to Seek God

IN THE EVERGREEN-FILLED MOUNTAINS of southern Oregon, my family owns a 150-year-old log cabin. A natural spring has been the water source for that cabin through many rainy and dry seasons for generations. Even when water wells on properties all around the area have gone dry, these underground springs of water have never stopped flowing to supply fresh water for us.

Spiritually speaking, we have access to never-ending streams of living water in our inner being. In the above verse, when Jesus spoke of the rivers of living water, it was the Holy Spirit living inside us He was speaking about. As believers, we already have access to an unlimited source of God's presence inside us.

However, sometimes our souls can feel desert dry as we struggle to find access to the living water springs of His presence. Classical Christian writer Jeanne Guyon says that to find God's presence is easier and more natural than taking a breath, we only need to know how and where to seek Him.[26]

---

[26] Jeanne Guyon, *Experiencing the Depths of Jesus Christ* (Sargent, GA: SeedSowers, 1996), 21-23.

The Kingdom is Within

"The Kingdom of God is within you!" (Luke 17:21). "You are a habitation" (Eph 2:22).

I found it a bit shocking at first to realize that we seek God in His kingdom, and His kingdom is within us. Sometimes it can be difficult for our carnal minds to understand the ways of the Spirit. But it is in your inner being that you will seek and find Him. Your Creator Father is a Spirit and made you spirit first then wrapped you in flesh. As a Christian believer, His Spirit dwells within you. You become His living temple on earth, a temple for the Holy Spirit. As the Scripture says, we have this treasure in earthen vessels.[27] We know Him in our hearts because our Creator Father deals with His creation through their hearts.

Revivalist and author Andrew Murray writes,

> If you see and feel nothing of God, it is because you seek Him in books, in the church, in outward religious exercises. You will not find Him there until you have first found Him in your heart. Seek Him in your heart, and you will never seek in vain, for He dwells there in His Holy Spirit!"[28]

As believers, His Spirit bears witness within our spirits that we are sons and daughters of God.[29] Our personal spirit knows His Spirit in our inner being.[30] Our personal spirit communes with the Spirit of God—spirit to Spirit in our inner being.

---

[27] 1 Cor 6:19; 2 Cor 4:7

[28] Andrew Murray, "Your Inner Life," *The Practice of God's Presence: Seven-in-One Anthology* (New Kensington, PA: Whitaker House, 2000), 470-472.

[29] Rom 8:15-16.

[30] Rom 8:15-16; John 14:16-18; 1 Cor 6:19; 2 Cor 4:7.

St. Augustine once said he "had lost much time in the beginning of his Christian experience by trying to find the Lord outwardly rather than by turning inwardly.[31] The difficulty lies in the fact that many people do not take notice of their own hearts. Classic Christian writer Francis Fenelon writes,

> When we bid men look for Thee in their own hearts. It is as though we bade them search for Thee in the remotest and most unknown lands! What territory is more distant or more unknown to the greater part of them, vain and dissipated as they are than the ground of their own hearts?
>
> Do they ever know what it is to enter within themselves? Have they ever endeavored to find the way? Can they even form the most distant conception of the nature of that interior sanctuary, that impenetrable depth of the soul where Thou desirest to be worshipped in spirit and in truth?[32]

Reformer John Calvin famously says that without knowledge of self, there is no knowledge of God, and without knowledge of God, there is no knowledge of self.[33] With knowledge of God comes knowledge of self. God's truth will expose hidden places in our hearts. Philosopher Blaise Pascal wrote, "Knowing God without knowing our wretchedness leads to pride. Knowing our wretchedness without knowing God leads to despair."[34]

---

[31] Quoted in Guyon, 11.

[32] Francois Fenelon, *The Inner Life*, Amazon Digital Services, Inc., Kindle Edition Location 107.

[33] Calvin, *Institutes of the Christian Religion*, 45-48.

[34] Blaise Pascal, *Pensees and Other Writings*, trans. H. Levi (Oxford: Oxford University Press, 1995), 64; quoted in Klaus Issler, *Wasting Time with God: A Christian Spirituality of Friendship with God* (Downers Grove, IL:

The Pharisees in Jesus's day knew the Bible well, yet they did not know their own hearts.

Do Not Neglect Inner Matters of the Heart

"Woe to you lawyers! For you have taken away the key of knowledge; you yourselves did not enter, and you hindered those who were entering" (Luke 11:52).

Jesus gave a stark warning to the Pharisees and experts in the law because they focused on the outside of the person rather than the heart. In fact, He chastised them for not entering the spiritual Kingdom of God and for standing in the way of others.

Jesus said they took away the *key that leads to knowledge of God*—by their focus on outward rather than inner matters of the heart. By focusing on the outward rituals alone, they hindered the people's access to the kingdom of God! They cleaned the outside of the cup but left the inner cup toxic. They did not take care of their inner temple, which was filled with pride and every such evil work. Jesus said they were like walking corpses, dead on the inside, because they were not aware of the inner life of their heart.

A great many churches give more time and attention to outward religious experiences than to the inward reality of the heart. Religious ceremonies are symbols that point people to Christ, and Christ dwells in our hearts by the Holy Spirit.

It is not the amount of effort we place in Bible study, although Bible study is important, or the number of prayers we pray, although prayer is important, or the number of good works we do, although those are important. However, honesty in our hearts is most important. The Father "who sees in secret" sees the inner secret chambers and communes with

InterVarsity Press, 2001), 147.

believers in the hidden places of the heart. Jesus states, "You foolish ones, did not He who made the outside make the inside also?"

As we develop in sensitivity toward God's Spirit, we also increase in sensitivity toward our own inner personal spirits/hearts. We learn to become more aware of our own sinfulness as we behold more of His holiness. His holy presence heals our inner corruption as we come honestly before Him, repent, and allow His Spirit to transform our spirits and souls. We are changed from glory to glory into the image of Christ.

"Behold, You desire truth in the innermost being, and in the hidden part You will make me know wisdom." Psalm 51:6 (TPT).
"I know that you delight to set your truth deep in my spirit. So, come into the hidden places of my heart and teach me wisdom" (Psalm 51: 6 NASB).

When God's Presence Doesn't Change Us

There are conditions, however, where people experience God's presence to a degree and are not changed. Sometimes there can be hindrances in a person's soul that keep them from seeing the truth of themselves or God's truths. One reason people do not change is they do not genuinely want to face God's light that shines and probes their interior life. They make excuses for fears, areas of unbelief, corrupt motives, and secret sins.

Author Rick Joyner shares some interesting revelation regarding this,

"To be changed into the image of the Lord, you must see His glory with an unveiled face. Excuses are the biggest veil that keep people from seeing Him as He is, and from seeing themselves as they are. Those with this veil do not change. Even if they see His glory it is distorted through the veil they wear, so they are not changed by it."[35]

Genuine intimacy in relationships, especially with God, will never flourish with excuses, distance, or deception in our hearts. A deeper relationship with God requires honesty in our innermost being.

If we are willing, His holiness will reveal the most wretched conditions in our hearts little by little, as we are able to face them without excuse. Then we must decide to change and ask for the courage to change. We must become honest before God and be willing to face the fear, unbelief, and evil in our own hearts. As it is written, "There is none righteous, not even one" (Rom 3:10).

The Palmist wrote, "Search me, O God, and know my heart; try me and know my anxious thoughts; and see if there be any hurtful [wicked, KJV] way in me, and lead me in the everlasting way" (Psa 139:23-34).

As believers, we depend on the blood of Jesus to forgive and cleanse us from all unrighteousness. Christ's sacrifice **does not excuse** wayward or hurtful ways in our hearts; however, **Jesus' blood does provide forgiveness, mercy, and grace to overcome.** The Holy Spirit will then lead and guide us into honesty in our hearts and actions.[36]

Knowing God intimately and growing in that relationship is a personal, inner, intuitive, and spiritual matter of our hearts. God desires to bring His healing light to the dark areas in our hearts.

---

[35] Rick Joyner, *The Path* (Fort Mill, SC: MorningStar Publications, 2013), 20.

[36] 1 John 1:9; John 16:13.

Cultivate God's Presence: The Honest Heart Prayer

"The heart is deceitful above all things and it is extremely sick; Who can understand it fully and know its secret motives?" (Jer 17:9 AMP).

Every so often at the natural spring on our family's property, we would clean around the source to make sure fallen limbs or sediment had not clogged up our flowing life source.

The same can be said regarding our personal Holy Spirit springs of living water. Sometimes it gets clogged with busyness, hurt, pain, bitterness, disappointments, and fears that need to be cleaned out.

Many people have a fervent desire to know God. In Jesus' time, the Pharisees had a fervent desire; Paul had a fervent desire. Yet many people's spiritual journey comes to a stop because they have not realized how necessary it is to give God permission to search their hearts.

We must be open to His work and ask Him to search our hearts. Then He will carefully and gently bring all our ugliness to the surface so that we have a chance to forgive, ask forgiveness, and be healed. We can trust Him with our hearts, for His blood will wash us clean and heal even the hidden areas we are afraid to see.

Honesty before God is the catalyst to becoming aware of our hearts and growing in our relationship with Him. He sees our hearts and knows the inner depths of our being better than we know ourselves. Your Creator God is holy, with not even a shadow of darkness in Him. His nature cannot come near sinful humanity until we are covered by Jesus' great sacrifice.

Suggested Prayer: Simply tell God you give Him permission to work in your heart. Ask Him to search your heart for anything opposed to Him and to bring healing. Pray Psalms 51:10, "Create in me a clean heart, O God; and renew a right spirit within me." You may sense some sin come to mind.

- Simply ask Him to forgive you. Give Him all your guilt, shame, fear, bitterness, unforgiveness, hurt, disappointment, anger, stress, failure, or any other thing that comes to mind.

- Ask Him to show you things in your heart that need forgiveness. He is faithful and just to forgive![37] Simply give those things to Him; they are too heavy for you to carry. Do that now.

- Forgive other people involved in your pain, hurt, or disappointment.

- Ask Him to take those things from your soul. You don't need those things in there. Get rid of them!

- Ask Jesus to bring healing to your mind, will, and emotions.

- Ask Him to fill you with expectation and excitement to discover His goodness in your life!

Now your ability for a deeper relationship is restored, and you are ready to experience greater depths of His presence and love! Awesome!

Important! You may or may not sense anything right at this moment, trust that God will bring things to you as you are ready to handle them, if

---

[37] 1 John 1:9.

not now then later. It is your heart that is surrendered to His working that is most important in this moment.

4 KNOWING GOD'S VOICE

BECAUSE WE CAN'T SEPARATE God's presence from His voice, we are going to look briefly at how we hear God speak to us in this section.

When I first decided I wanted to pursue God's presence and hear God speak to me, I didn't know how to recognize God's voice or what God's voice sounded like. I bought lots of books and sermons looking for answers. The general advice I got was, "You will know when you know," or "Keep reading your Bible and you will hear Him." Although this advice was true, it was not helpful to me at first.

There are some simple, yet profound, keys I found in my journey that helped my progress tremendously. Thus, you can learn from my struggle, and your experience will be smoother. You can reap the benefits of my study, and it won't take you so long to understand how to hear God's voice more clearly and practice His presence!

I also discovered along the way that hearing God is not just for pastors, preachers, and special spiritual people out there! Jesus said, "My sheep hear my voice." **So, because you are a sheep, you can learn to hear God's voice clearly.**

You can learn what God's voice sounds like and recognize when He speaks to you! Below are some keys I trust will be helpful.

Paying Attention

A major part of hearing God speak is a result of paying attention. In an age of multimedia and multitasking, many people have difficulty being aware enough to hear God's message. Most people need to deliberately practice listening to become aware of the subtle ways God communicates.

It is not that God cannot be heard. If God wants His creation to hear, we will hear. Sometimes God does grab people's attention by shouting at them. However, to grow in intimacy with God requires we recognize a more subtle conversation, as well as the shout.

What Does God's Voice Sound Like?

Jesus said, "My sheep hear My voice, and I know them, and they follow Me" (John 10:27).

All believers are equipped with spiritual ears to hear and spiritual eyes to see. Yet not all believers hear and see. There is an internet video floating around where a sheep runs headlong into a trench. We watch the owner grab the leg of the sheep, pull, and pull until the errant sheep is plucked out of the trench only for it to run off and run directly back into the trench again.

The Bible says the rebellious do not see. Some sheep are headstrong and do not see. But you, my friends, are not like the rebellious ones. We are the ones who open our eyes to embrace our Lord and His Words to us.[38] For He is a communicating God who spoke in times past and continues to speak today.

God Communicates to Our Personal Spirit

God communicates by His Holy Spirit to our personal human spirit. He can communicate in different ways, yet all are from the same Spirit of God.[39]

---

[38] Deut 29:4; Ezek 12:2.

[39] Heb 1:1-2; 1 Cor 12.

When we first awake to notice spiritual things, they will be very subtle, because the Holy Spirit speaks differently than our logical mind normally notices. We must ask and expect to notice more. Here are some of the varieties of ways He might communicate with our personal spirits.[40] He can speak:

- through the Scriptures
- in an audible voice
- in a gentle whisper
- through sensing His flowing thoughts in our personal spirit
- through peace and love
- through visions, dreams, and pictures that come to mind
- through apostles, prophets, pastors, teachers, evangelists
- through the gifts of the Holy Spirit
- through circumstances (think Jonah)
- through emotions and/or a knowing in our personal spirit
- through other people
- through angels
- through songs
- through devotional books
- through a donkey (Balaam)
- or through any other means He sees fit

God uses all these different ways to communicate directly to our human spirit through His Holy Spirit. There are some things He can only reveal through His Spirit to our personal human spirits in our inner being.[41]

It is in the inner being that Adam and Eve understood God's love and commands. In their heart, they communicated with their Creator spirit-

---

[40] Acts 2:17; Gal 5:22-23; 1 Cor 12:10; Ps 77:6; John 7:38; Rom 8:14; Luke 24:32.

[41] 1 Cor 2:9-10.

to-Spirit. In the beginning, their hearts were not contaminated by sin. They were without fear or disappointment. No walls separated the heart-to-heart communication with their Creator Father.

The experience of recognizing and hearing our Creator God in our inner spirit is of paramount importance to developing a deeper relationship with Him. We learn to sense how He communicates with us personally in our inner being (heart).

When we spend time with someone in our personal relationships, we get to know more about them. They gradually reveal more and more about themselves. The same is true with our Lord. As we spend time with Him, we learn to recognize the ways He communicates, and he reveals more about Himself.

He does speak apart from the Bible, but never in contradiction to the Bible.

In fact, a major way the Spirit speaks to believers is through the illumination of the Scriptures. The Spirit of revelation causes the words in the Bible to come to life to become the living voice of God to us. His voice continues to speak revealing Christ afresh.

All revelations of the Spirit will align with the Scriptures and magnify the Scripture's authority. In fact, the Holy Spirit's communication will enhance and confirm the Bible to believers' hearts. God loves to reveal Himself to us—His beloved people— in a variety of ways.

Hearing God's Audible Voice

When we talk about hearing God's voice, people generally think about hearing God's audible voice, like we hear one another. Saul, who became the Apostle Paul, in Acts 9, heard the audible voice of God on the road to Damascus, and the men with him also heard the voice. So, God does speak audibly, and maybe he has spoken audibly to you or others you know, but He also uses various other forms of communication as well.

There have been a couple of times I have heard God speak so loudly that it could have been loud enough for others to hear. I remember one time God spoke so loudly I thought everyone around me heard. I was standing in the Oral Roberts University cafeteria, and it felt like lightning went through me. I fell into my chair and my lunch tray hit the table. I looked around, but no one else seemed to hear. If God had wanted them to hear, they would have heard, but the message was for me alone. You probably have some great stories of your own about hearing God, I would love to hear some of them. You can email me if you like.

In this book, I want to focus on those other times when His voice is harder to discern. We can increase our awareness of His voice to understand the myriad ways He communicates with us as His children.

Hearing God In Spontaneous Flowing Thoughts

For the Father loves the Son and shows Him all things that He Himself is doing; and the Father will show Him greater works than these, so that you will be amazed (John 5:20).

One of the major ways God communicates to His children personally is through spontaneous flowing thoughts that come to mind. It may sometimes feel like words that bubble up from the Holy Spirit inside.[42] You may hear people say, "an impression or thought came to me," "I sense the Lord saying." His voice can be described as "a subtle thought not my own," or "a gentle whisper; a still small voice."[43]

These God thoughts are not premeditated by us but are spontaneous and unprompted thoughts that come to mind. He may bring a specific word or situation to mind that did not come as the result of a detailed thought process. Jesus, himself, lived from an inner flow of thoughts and

---

[42] 1 Cor 2:9-10.

[43] 1 Kings 19:12.

pictures from His Father, spiritually hearing and seeing what His Father was doing.[44]

We humans have logical progressive thought patterns where one thought is connected to another thought and then another. God's thoughts flow as spontaneous or unprompted ideas that come to our minds, especially during a time of prayer or meditation on the Word. When you hear God's voice, you will generally "hear" His thoughts inside your mind. You may or may not hear Him audibly.

An Example of How to Recognize God's Voice as Flowing Thoughts

As an example, we may look at the clock and see it is noon. We think, "Oh I am hungry; what is there to eat; there are some cookies on the counter; no I should eat lunch, not cookies; but what can I have; maybe there is some lunch meat; no we ate all the lunch meat; maybe peanut butter; do we have chips left; fruit?"

Do you see? Our human thoughts follow a pattern from one thing to the next.

When you begin to hear God's voice to you, you may look at the clock and see it is noon.

Then He will drop a thought into your mind like, "I will take care of all your needs, just as I said I would."

God's thoughts flow peacefully and easily to you in the first person with "I" statements. Then you will feel His love and care and probably tear up.

We can recognize that our human thoughts flow in a reasoned, logical thought progression, but God's thoughts to us flow unexpectedly. So, what this means is you must be open to little interruptions in your regular

---

[44] John 5:19-20, 30.

thought flow and begin to recognize spontaneous flowing thoughts that come to you.

God's Words Will Be Expressed Through Our Own Personality

Sometimes, God's voice will sound a lot like your thoughts, but you will know they did not come from you. His thoughts will be wiser, more healing, more loving, and more concerned about your motive than your own personal thoughts. God's thoughts are expressed through your own personal style and speech, just as we can see each of the Gospel writer's personalities came through in their writings.

God Can Speak To Our Hearts Through Songs

"He will rejoice over you with gladness, He will quiet you with His love, He will rejoice over you with singing" (Zeph 3:17 NKJV).

God can use praise and worship songs as another in the variety of ways He communicates to us. When I was the director of a faith-based rehabilitation center, a teacher arrived harried and late for class one day. So, to give her a minute to collect herself, I began the class with a song that "came" to my mind. After class, the teacher said the song calmed and reassured her. Additionally, this song had comforted her all her life, and as a child, she had the words of this particular song posted on her bedroom wall.

This way of "hearing" God may be a bit different than most, but I pay attention when I wake up with a song in my mind, or if a song just "comes" to me that I haven't been thinking about. When this happens, the words of the song will have been just the words I needed to hear at that moment to comfort or reassure me. These kinds of interactions with the Holy Spirit are not by accident. He knows our hearts and lives so intricately and wants to minister to us in meaningful ways that comfort our souls.

God's Voice Will Cause A Special Reaction Inside You

God's thoughts will cause a special reaction inside you. They will cause excitement, conviction, faith, life, awe, wonder, joy, love, and peace. God's voice does not sound like negative or accusing thoughts. Those are not from God.

When you embrace God's thoughts, there is grace, strength, and joy to carry His thoughts and words out.

As you become more and more sensitive to God's thoughts and communications to you, you train your spiritual senses to discern good and evil more effectively.

Your loving Lord begins to share more insight about day-to-day situations with you because you are His friend. You will hear God give you divine strategies for your life and your family's lives. He will help you with wisdom and understanding in all areas of your life.

> *"Call to me and I will answer you, and will tell you great and hidden things that you have not known"* (Jeremiah 33:3 ESV).

God's Voice Can Be Subtle

Unless He shouts at you, you will hear God's thoughts as soothing, gentle, and peaceful. His voice is easily cut off by stress or exertion of our self-will. So, don't get frustrated or stressed trying hard. Relax.

Most people find they learn to hear God more clearly when they practice being still or quiet, which we will talk about more in the next section. The best stance is to relax and be at rest. Trust God's goodness and provision, no matter what your circumstance. Trust His goodness toward you whether you sense anything special or not at this moment. Recognizing God's presence and hearing His voice is a journey of knowing Him more intimately, and you are on a journey. So give all your experiences or non-experiences to Him, and be at peace.

Discerning God's Voice Versus Satan's Voice

A common way to hear God's voice is by recognizing His thoughts toward us and distinguishing them from other thoughts. We can learn to discern which thoughts come from our own soul, versus thoughts from God or thoughts from the enemy. Life is easier when we can identify the source of thoughts in our minds.

Remember the following principles to help distinguish God's thoughts from satan's or our own.

- God's thoughts will come to mind spontaneously. God's thoughts are not our normal cognitive analytical process. When we normally think about a thing, we move from one idea to the next, then the next. When you receive God's thoughts, it will seem like an idea or thought just dropped into your mind.

- God's thoughts flow easily and are expressed in first person. For example, Jeremiah writes, "The Lord has appeared of old to me, saying: 'Yes, I have loved you with an everlasting love; therefore, with lovingkindness, I have drawn you.'"[45]

- God's thoughts will be expressed through your own personal style and speech, just as each of the Gospel writers' personalities came through in their writings. However, His thoughts to you will never contradict His written words in the Bible. God's thoughts will always point to Scripture.

---

[45] Jer 31:3 (NKJV).

- God's thoughts will be wiser, more healing, more loving, and more concerned about your inner heart motive than your own personal thoughts.
- Although God can shout at you, most often His thoughts are light and gentle, easily cut off by any exertion of personal self-will.
- God's thoughts will cause a special quickening reaction inside your spirit. They will cause excitement, conviction, faith, life, awe, joy, love, and peace. The thoughts of the Spirit of God will be evident by good fruit.[46] Negative or accusing thoughts are not God.
- When you embrace God's thoughts, there is grace, strength, encouragement, and joy to carry out His thoughts and words.

The following are characteristics of satan's voice to your mind:
- Satan's thoughts and temptations appeal to your fleshly desires rather than God's principles. In other words, he presents thoughts that tempt you to fulfill a legitimate need in an ungodly way.
- Satan's thoughts barrage your mind to pressure you into action.
- Satan's thoughts highlight the things you do not have, rather than the awesome things you do have. They compare you to others and tell you that you are not good enough.
- His thoughts are negative and accusing.
- His thoughts tempt you to doubt and fear.
- They tempt you to complain and be unthankful and bitter.
- They are stressful and confusing.

---

[46] Gal 5:22-23.

- Satan's thoughts may have a bit of truth but are twisted to imply something else entirely. His thoughts cause you to question what you know to be Biblically right.
- Satan's thoughts twist God's principles to bring doubt and distance into our relationship with our Creator and others.

As you continue to recognize the difference between God's thoughts, satan's thoughts, and your own thoughts, you train your spiritual senses to choose the path of love, joy, and peace more often.[47]

---

[47] 2 Cor 10:4-5.

Cultivate God's Presence: Reflect on Discerning

1. Reflect on the previous items. Which ones stand out to you? Did any of these items take you by surprise?
2. Was there anything listed that you did not know?
3. What else would you add to this list?
4. How will these principles change how you listen to the thoughts in your mind?
5. Take time to reflect on the thoughts you have had during this day. Can you distinguish God's thoughts from satan's thoughts?

Easily Hear God's Voice

The following exercise will guide you step by step to practice hearing God's voice more clearly and extensively for yourself. If you don't think you've ever heard God's voice, or even if you already hear God's voice, you can grow to a greater degree in your experience with Him!

I am offering this strategy because it is specifically designed to help you hear God's voice clearly.

God communicates in many ways, yet I find that I receive more details and longer words from God in this manner than any other way of hearing God. Every person has a different personality and temperament, and everyone experiences things differently. Some people hear God immediately, and others, like me, need more practice. However, I have seen everyone who has tried this method experience God in profound ways not previously experienced.

This is a type of journaling that is easy to do. It is a Biblical method that can help you grow in discerning the voice of God to you. It is simply recording your prayers and then writing what you sense to be the answer from God. It is a discussion between you and God. We see David did the same thing in the Psalms. Many times, he would pour out his feelings and requests to God, and then in the process of writing, his attitude would shift from despair to praise, hope, and expectation. Through the ages, it is easy to see that the Psalms were inspired and prophetic Words from God.

The reason journaling helps so much is that you can simply write whatever spontaneously comes to mind without judging. There is always time to judge later.

Personally, when I feel like I am not hearing God about something, I go to this method. For some reason, our brain hinders hearing God in our spirit, so writing with God breaks through these mental barriers. Writing focuses the brain on the writing process and allows our personal spirit to communicate with God's Spirit without hindering the process.

Cultivate God's Presence: Hearing God Through Journaling

These simple steps are taken from Habakkuk 2:1-3 and Rev 1:10-11.[48] I suggest you use this proven process when you begin. You may have to refer to these steps a few times at first.

Exercise Steps:

Step 1. Quiet Down & Focus

Be still and quiet yourself to hear His voice. Psalm 46:10 tells us to "Cease striving [let go, relax] and know that I am God." The King James version renders this, "Be still, and know that I am God."

Set your mind on Jesus and focus on the truth of Jesus Christ in some manner (a Scripture, Christian music, a picture of Him in your mind, a prayer phrase, the cross, the empty tomb, or something that helps focus your mind on Jesus).

For this time, you can use this verse, "I have loved you with an everlasting love; Therefore, I have drawn you with lovingkindness" (Jer 31:3).

---

[48] Mark Virkler and Patti Virkler, *Four Keys to Hearing God's Voice* (Shippensburg, PA: Destiny Image, 2010), 49-50. I first learned this method from Mark Virkler and have adapted their method for our use here.

If you have trouble quieting your mind, read the Scripture verse very slowly and take in every word until your mind is quiet. If you still have trouble stilling your mind, jump to the next section "When It's Hard to Be Still."

Step 2. Ask Questions

Write your question, "Lord, what would you say to me about _____?" For this first time ask, "Lord, what would you say to me about how much You love me?"

Step 3. Listen & Write

Recognize God's voice as spontaneous flowing thoughts that come to your mind. Begin to notice that your thoughts are analytical and progress logically from one thing to the next. Yet, remember thoughts from God are spontaneous, flowing from His Holy Spirit living inside you.[49]

Simply write the flow of thoughts and/or pictures that come to your mind after you have asked Him a question. Just let the words flow and write!

What to Expect

When you begin to hear God's voice in this manner, you will find He will speak healing, love, and affirmation. He will speak edification, exhortation, and comfort to your heart.[50] He will bring love, encouragement, and self-acceptance.

In time, this type of journaling may flow into gifts of the Holy Spirit, such as prophecy, word of wisdom, word of knowledge, etc.

Additionally, you should have a solid knowledge of the Bible, because all *rhema* words (spontaneous God-words) will be built upon the *logos* words (written) in the Bible and tested against the Bible.

---

[49] 2 Cor 10:4-5; Gal 2:20; John 7:37-39.
[50] 1 Cor 14:3.

This style of expressing your feelings to God is an effective strategy for personal spiritual and emotional growth. You should also have a couple of trusted spiritual mentors/friends to help and support you in your journey.

For Those Hesitant to Write

If you feel you write too slowly, it is ok. God knows this and will accommodate you. Do it anyway. Just try it right here and now. I had apprehensions the first time I did this too. I did not want to write. But I got past those feelings when I began to experience the Lord speaking to me in this way.

Just write, do not worry about if it is from God or not. After you are finished writing, then you can judge what you wrote.

Writing focuses the brain on the writing process and allows your personal spirit to communicate with God's Spirit without hindering the process.

Even if You Hear God Already

You may hear God already. That is super great. This method has allowed me to hear better and receive more from God than ever before. Before I heard phrases from God, but now I can hear paragraphs and pages. If this exercise seemed too easy, ask the Lord to show you deeper depths of this practice. We can learn to hear God in the quiet, so that we can hear Him in the noise of life and practice His presence 24/7. The following exercises will continue to help you develop new relationship skills to experience His goodness in greater dimensions.

Another Benefit

Another benefit of learning this skill is that if you write what the Lord is saying to you, you can refer back to this later for understanding and encouragement.

For example, I wrote some things in my journal; and at the time, I did not fully understand what I was receiving. Six months later I reread what I had written and understood it completely. In fact, I was amazed by the Lord's glorious ways. This built my faith in God and drew me closer to Him.

My Prayer for You: Dear Lord, By the power of the blood of Jesus, I break off all negative words and lies that suggest my friend cannot write or that journal writing is too hard.

These are lies of the enemy. We repent for coming into agreement with them and proclaim that we can do all things through Christ who strengthens us.

God, I ask you to give us creative, healing, and compassionate words of love. We choose to hear these words and record them. We are excited to be a part of sharing Your love, creativity, and intimacy.

I ask You Lord to silence every fear and hindrance in Jesus' name. I ask for the Spirit of wisdom and revelation in the knowledge of Christ to guide these dear readers. Thank you, Lord! Amen.

P.S. Spelling and grammar are not important in this journal writing exercise. If someone in your past has made writing difficult…forgive them.

Now, stop and do the exercise!

When It Is Hard To Be Still

"There is always music amongst the trees in the garden, but our hearts must be very quiet to hear it." ~ Minnie Aumonier

I was at a retreat years ago where the leader asked the entire assembly to be still, quiet down, and write what we thought the Lord was speaking to us. I did not know what to do or how to do it. I did not know how to quiet the anxious thoughts in my mind—much less hear what God would say to me.

As instrumental music played quietly, I fumbled with the paper; I fumbled with the pen; I fumbled with my jeans, and I fumed. I questioned how we could be asked to just sit there.

Just to get to the retreat center, I left a difficult situation. I left my child. I left a multitude of things undone. The travel was long, hard, and frustrating, and my mind was going in a million different directions. I thought we could just sing, listen to a sermon, sleep in, and eat a few fancy meals I did not have to cook. That's what I paid for—or so I thought. That was my attitude at the time.

Since then, I have learned "how" to quiet my soul, find peace, and sense His presence in prayer. This is a super simple process that helped me, and I am certain it will help you also! You can learn how to quiet your mind and receive hope and peace from God in any circumstance. You can live in the verse that says, "Be still and know that I am God."

Learn To Quiet Your Soul and Be Still

"God is our refuge and strength,
A very present help in trouble.
Therefore we will not fear, though the earth should change
There is a river whose streams make glad the city of God,
The holy dwelling places of the Most High.

[Cease striving] Be still and know that I am God;
I will be exalted among the nations; I will be exalted in the
earth"
(Psalm 46:1, 2, 4, 10).

Psalms 46 gives us hope for peace in the middle of life's troubles. We will take a moment to explore the Psalm as a guide for how to bring peace to our anxious and troubled thoughts.

Of course, the most famous line is verse one, "God is our refuge and strength, a very present help in trouble."[51] Sometimes we can acknowledge these wonderful promises and not understand how to access the help our Lord promises.

Verse 10 says, "Be still and know that I am God!" It is interesting that the Hebrew verb translated "be still" means to stop, be inactive, let go, and relax. This verb is a command to readers and is also translated "cease striving," "surrender," "stop," "desist," and "make peace."[52]

When we are surrounded by worries, our God is bigger than any troubling circumstance we encounter. He is larger than our enemies; He is greater than our troubled hearts; He is our fortress with abundant supplies!

The Problem for Us

The problem is that sometimes we are overwhelmed by worries, fears, and pain and it is hard for us to access the peace we are meant to live

---

[51] As an interesting side note, Martin Luther's famous hymn translated, "A Mighty Fortress Is Our God" is based on his paraphrase of Psalm 46.

[52] R. G. Bratcher and W. D. Reyburn, "Psalm 46:10," *A Translator's Handbook on The Book of Psalms* (New York: United Bible Societies, 1991), 435.

from. Psalm 46 gives us a clue on how to do that. It says our human response to overwhelming troubles should be to "be still and know."

In other words, we are to cease striving so hard in our own will and ways, and simply stop and be still, and surrender the moment to God and His dealings–to be still and know He is God.

Often, we hold tightly to our own opinions, without stopping to hear God's opinion. We hold on to our hurt, pain, and bitterness. We grow impatient with others. We are caught up in our thoughts, emotions, fears, offenses, attitudes, and worries, and we lose any sense of stillness, peace, love, or joy.

Yet, the verse commands us to let go, relax, be still, cease striving and surrender to God's will and ways. St. Augustine asked, "to what purpose are we emphatically commanded to 'be still?' We are commanded to be still so that we may see that God would say, 'I am God. That is, not you, but I am God. I created, I create anew; I formed, I form anew; I made, I make anew.'"[53]

We cannot see the majesty of our mighty God or His goodness to us when we are caught up in our worries, scurrying around with anxious, angry thoughts. Our Lord implores us to cast all our cares on Him, for they are too heavy a load for us to carry. God has the answers to our problems and peace for our souls, but we miss His comfort in our emotional flurry. Thus, the command to be still.

> *"Be anxious for nothing, but in everything by prayer and supplication with thanksgiving let your requests be made known to God" (Phil 4:6).*

---

[53] Augustine of Hippo. *Expositions on the Book of Psalms*, (1888). In P. Schaff (Ed.), A. C. Coxe (Trans.), Saint Augustin: *Expositions on the Book of Psalms*, Vol. 8 (New York: Christian Literature Company), 160.

The Value of a Still Mind/Soul

The value of learning to be still and quiet was pointed out to Elijah in the cave at Mt. Horeb. God often says to His people, "What do you see?" and "What do you hear?" And this day God invited Elijah to witness and learn. Elijah witnessed a great and strong wind that tore apart mountains and shattered rocks. Then an earthquake shook the earth, and a fire raged.

But after this massive display of power and might, Elijah recognized a still small voice—a gentle breeze, a gentle whisper.

God wanted Elijah to learn to recognize the breeze of His presence, the gentle moving of His Spirit, His whisper. God communicates in various ways, and this time God wanted Elijah to learn to recognize Him in the quiet and still calmness (1 Kings 19:9-13).

In quiet and stillness of soul, we too can recognize the Spirit of God and see His mighty greatness.

We can learn to cease our striving and rest in God's ability and desire to be our Savior. He is the One with the ideas, plans, solutions, and wisdom for all our circumstances. We can trust Him who is able to make all grace abound to us for His glory.

When we find Him in quietness and trust, we find everything we need.[54] We learn to trust Him enough to "be still and know He is God."

An Example of Learning Quiet Your Soul

Hearing about other people's experiences helps us to grow in our own experiences. Here is a good example from A.B. Simpson that illustrates the struggles we encounter in trying to quiet our souls.

> A score of years ago, a friend placed in my hand a book called True Peace. It was an old medieval message, and it

---

[54] Is 30:15.

had but one thought—*that God was waiting in the depths of my being to talk to me if I would only get still enough to hear His voice.*

I thought this would be a very easy matter, and so began to get still. But I had no sooner commenced than a perfect pandemonium of voices reached my ears, a thousand clamoring notes from without and within, until I could hear nothing but their noise and din. Some were my own voices, my own questions, some my very prayers.

Others were suggestions of the tempter and the voices from the world's turmoil. In every direction I was pulled and pushed and greeted with noisy acclamations and unspeakable unrest.

It seemed necessary for me to listen to some of them and to answer some of them; but God said, "Be still and know that I am God." Then came the conflict of thoughts for tomorrow, and its duties and cares; but God said, "Be still."

And as I listened, and slowly learned to obey, and shut my ears to every sound, I found after a while that when the other voices ceased, or I ceased to hear them, there was a still small voice in the depths of my being that began to speak with an inexpressible tenderness, power and comfort.

As I listened, it became to me the voice of prayer, the voice of wisdom, the voice of duty, and I did not need to think so hard, or pray so hard, or trust so hard; but that "still small voice" of the Holy Spirit in my heart was God's prayer in my secret soul, was God's answer to all my questions, was God's life and strength for soul and body, and became the substance of all knowledge, and all prayer and all blessing: for it was the living GOD Himself as my life, my all.

It is thus that our spirit drinks in the life of our risen Lord, and we go forth to life's conflicts and duties like a flower that has drunk in, through the shades of night, the cool and crystal drops of dew. But as dew never falls on a stormy night, so the dews of His grace never come to the restless soul. —A. B. Simpson[55]

[55] *Streams In the Desert,* June 30 Public domain content taken from *Streams in the Desert* by Mrs. Charles Cowman. YouDevotion© 2016 Tap Tap Studio http://www.youdevotion.com/streams/june/30 (accessed July 8, 2018).

Cultivate God's Presence: How to Quiet Your Mind

Since it is extremely difficult to hear what God is saying and experience His presence when we are anxious and upset, we must learn how to be still and quiet on the inside.

For this exercise, we use a verse of Scripture to specifically train our minds to be still. In the beginning, you will have many thoughts and emotions racing through your mind. But if you focus on a Scripture verse in this specific way, the Word Himself will still your mind and reveal Himself to you.

Please note, we do not empty our minds. We are not emptying our minds so that any old thing can fill them.

In the past, we may have surrendered our minds to random thoughts, but this is an exercise in surrendering our minds to Christ alone.[56] We set our minds on things above.[57] We set our minds on our Savior, Jesus Christ.

This exercise helps us discipline our minds to focus on Jesus through His Word.

---

[56] Rom 6:16.

[57] Col 3:1-3.

Find a comfortable place free of distractions and have your Bible and a writing tablet handy. You may want to play some Christian music. If you do play music, play instrumental Christian music (without words) for this exercise, because your mind will start focusing on the words of the song—which is fine usually, but that is not the goal in this exercise.

There are different methods you can use to still your soul, but for this exercise, we want to learn to use the Holy Scriptures to still your mind and teach you to focus on God's presence.

- If you think of things you need to do, write them down to deal with later.
- If you have thoughts about sin in your life, confess that to God and ask for forgiveness.
- If your mind is flitting about, focus only on the Scripture verse and/or picture Jesus with you in your mind.[58]

My Prayer for You: Dear Lord, I thank you for your rich mercy and great love with which You have loved us. Even when we were dead in our sins, you made us alive together with Christ by grace and raised us up with Him and seated us in the heavenly places in Christ Jesus.[59]

I ask you to forgive my friends for missing the mark in any way. I ask you to surround them right now with Your love and peace; silence all the noise in their mind and soothe their emotions. Break them free from all negative preconceived ideas associated with Your Word. I ask for Your peace to envelop Your children at this moment. Teach them to be still and know You are with them. Thank you, Lord.

---

[58] Heb 13:5.

[59] Eph 2:5-6.

Exercise Steps:

Step 1. Pick A Scripture of Prayer or Praise

For this first exercise, you can use a verse from Psalm 46, which I have listed below, or The Lord's Prayer in Matthew 6:9-11. Any verse of prayer or praise is a good place to start.

Focus verse: Psalm 46

1 God is our refuge and strength,

A very present help in trouble.

2 Therefore we will not fear, though the earth should change

And though the mountains slip into the heart of the sea;

3 Though its waters roar and foam,

Though the mountains quake at its swelling pride. Selah.

4 There is a river whose streams make glad the city of God,

The holy dwelling places of the Most High.

5 God is in the midst of her, she will not be moved;

God will help her when morning dawns.

6 The nations made an uproar, the kingdoms tottered;

He raised His voice, the earth melted.

7 The Lord of hosts is with us;

The God of Jacob is our stronghold. Selah.

8 Come, behold the works of the Lord,

Who has wrought desolations in the earth?

9 He makes wars to cease to the end of the earth;

He breaks the bow and cuts the spear in two;

He burns the chariots with fire.

10 "Cease striving and know that I am God;

I will be exalted among the nations; I will be exalted in the earth."

11 The Lord of hosts is with us;

The God of Jacob is our stronghold. Selah

Step 2. Pray This Suggested or Similar Prayer

Dear Lord, I ask you to forgive me for coming short of the life you ordained for me. I ask you to meet me in Your Word, still my mind and teach me of You. Thank you.

Step 3. Read the Scripture

Read very slowly, one phrase or word at a time, until you experience a sense of peace, then stay in this experience as long as you feel His peace.

The Word will quiet your mind and bring peace. The Scripture is for focus in this particular exercise so that your mind does not stray.

Our goal here is to use the Scripture to learn to quiet our soul (mind, will, emotions), and acquire the habit of setting our minds on things above. Simply begin by faith that the Word will still your soul.

Breathe in the Holy Spirit. Breathe out all anxiety. Wait in His presence and take into your heart the loving peace of the moment. Notice the peace.

Continue waiting until the sense of His presence lifts, then move to the next phrase. As you learn to set your mind on the Word in this way, you will begin to experience His divine presence. You may or may not get through the entire Psalm. Be at peace whatever your experience with the Lord of the Psalm.

If you continue to practice this skill, you will be able to use this strategy to bring peace to your soul any time you feel out of peace. What you experience with Jesus in these moments is powerful!

This peaceful presence is the living river whose streams make glad the city of God, which flows from the dwelling places of the Most High (verse 4). Here our anxious thoughts turn to praise. It is in the peaceful praise of our hearts we recognize the river of living water flowing from our inner being as Jesus talks about.

Here we drink and are satisfied. The river of His presence brings healing to our spirit, soul (mind, will, emotions), and body!

Step 4. Write

Write down any spontaneous thoughts that come to your mind in your notebook/journal. This simple act validates your experience in your mind and helps sort through your experiences. You may want to share with a trusted, supportive friend if appropriate.

I encourage you to practice this exercise every day for many days—until it becomes easy and familiar. It takes a bit of practice to learn a new skill, so do not be discouraged if your first attempt is not what you expect! You may want to refer back to this exercise until this practice becomes a habit. Keep pursuing Jesus in this way.

If you continue the practice, you will gain more and more confidence; and Jesus will share more of Himself with you. You will learn to experience greater depths of His love.

If this exercise was difficult, do not give up! The presence of God heals, brings peace, and sorts out all the pieces of our lives. If this exercise was easy for you, ask the Lord to show you deeper depths of this same skill. He will do so.

> *And without faith it is impossible to please Him, for he who comes to God must believe that He is and that He is a rewarder of those who seek Him (Heb 11:6).*

I pray for you dear reader that you would practice this little exercise to find God in amazing new ways in your life!

Learning how to still your soul is the important first step in learning to practice the presence of God. In the above exercise, we learned to use the Scripture to come to a place where we feel a sense of peace and inner stillness in the Lord's presence. Continue that exercise until it becomes easy for you to feel His sweet peaceful presence. Then make this exercise a part of your life.

5 KNOWING GOD'S PRESENCE IN WORSHIP

"In worship, God imparts himself to us." — *C.S. Lewis*

WHILE DOING RESEARCH IN GENESIS, I found some interesting insight regarding worship God instituted at the very beginning of human history that might be helpful in pursuits here. In this light, we will explore worship and praise and how it factors into knowing God's presence more intimately.

The Holy Temple of God

"Then the Lord God took the man and put him into the garden of Eden" (Gen 2:15).

East of Eden God created a sacred garden and "put" (sometimes translated "placed") Adam and Eve inside its borders. The word "put/placed" when literally translated from the original language means "set to rest" (Gen 2:8,15).[60] God created and put our first parents into a specific and set apart garden in Eden. You might remember that satan had already been cast down from heaven. Thus, Adam and Eve were put

---

[60]A. P. Ross, "Genesis," vol 1, ed. J. F. Walvoord & R. B. Zuck, *The Bible Knowledge Commentary: An Exposition of the Scriptures* (Wheaton, IL: Victor Books, 1985), 31.

in a safe, sacred, and restful place of fellowship in their Creator's peaceful presence.[61]

This word translated "put" here is also the same word used for an item dedicated before the presence of the Lord.[62] Adam and Eve were put/placed in the sacred Garden of God's presence and set apart as dedicated and holy. The Garden in Eden was a set apart and consecrated place where God could dwell with His creation in precious worship, communication, and fellowship.[63]

The Garden was a symbolic precursor for what would later come to be known as the tent of the tabernacle and then later the temple. All the symbolism of the Garden repeats in the tabernacle and temple.

The temple was a set apart, sacred place built according to God's specific instructions where His presence could fill the space and dwell with His people. In the temple, He could be at home with His children as He was in the Garden of Eden.

The original Garden was a specific space where heaven came down to earth, a place where God's will was done on earth as it is in heaven. We could also say this was the ideal location where heaven uniquely interfaced with the earth.

The Garden was the ideal place of unhindered intimate fellowship and worship, a place of instant and easy access to God's presence. It was the at-home space with God that Adam and Eve understood.

Adam and Eve knew pure, holy unhindered adoration from their hearts. In this atmosphere, His glorious presence was easily recognized and instinctively evoked gratitude, adoration, and praise.

---

[61] Gen 3:8.

[62] K. A. Mathews, *The New American Commentary*, vol. 1A (Nashville, TN: Broadman & Holman Publishers, 1996), 208-209.

[63] I write about this more in depth in *Return to Eden*, 12.

Of course, Adam and Eve lived the ideal life of worship in God's presence until sin entered to spoil the relationship. However, God covered Adam and Eve with slain animal skins and instituted animal sacrifice as the temporary blood sacrifice until Jesus Christ came as the ultimate sacrifice, for "without the shedding of blood there is no forgiveness."[64]

In God's love for His children, He provided this plan to atone for humanity's sin so that as a Holy God He could continue intimate fellowship with His sin-laden children.

The Bible tells us that Adam and Eve lived in the original sanctuary of God. Yet today, each Christian believer is a living sanctuary. You are a holy and dedicated living temple of God with the Holy Spirit living within you. You are a sacred temple of God!

Even today, worship and pure adoration in our hearts will usher us into the ancient sanctuary of God's presence. Our worship is not limited to a certain place, style, or time of day. We have access to God's eternal kingdom in the Spirit, inside our hearts, twenty-four hours a day, seven days a week. Here we can give him the glory he deserves, and we can come to know God's presence intimately through worship in the holy temple of our hearts.

"Do you not know that you are a temple of God and that the Spirit of God dwells in you?" (1 Cor 3:16).

---

[64] Heb 9:22.

The Door of Thanksgiving and Praise

"Enter his gates with thanksgiving and his courts with praise"
(Psalm 100:4).
"You are holy, O You who are enthroned upon [inhabit] the
praises of Israel" (Psalm 22:3).

As you continue to grow in awareness of your Lord's presence, you will develop the skill to connect with His presence at any time in worship. It is in moments of praise and worship that many people first feel their Creator Father's loving manifest presence.

We can enter the Garden of God's presence today only because of Jesus' sacrifice, even though sin will try to hinder us. Others may try to access the kingdom of Heaven by other means, but they are but thieves and robbers.[65] There is no other way except The Way, Jesus Christ!

The Gateway into His Presence

You probably recognize the verse above (Psalm 100:4) from popular praise songs. The verse clearly references the tabernacle plan and access to God's presence. We see praise is linked closely with thanksgiving and is, in fact, the gate or access point into His presence. Thanksgiving is the state of mind that releases praise. In other words, praise comes from our heart of gratitude. The more gratitude we develop in our hearts, the deeper we are able to connect with God in praise. In gratitude, we make more room for Him in the residence of our hearts. A negative and complaining heart hinders our access.

However, as Psalm 22:3, listed above, indicates God inhabits or takes up residence in the place where praise dwells. The Lord lives in the middle of praise. Of course, Heaven is a place of continual worship of God, both day and night.[66] So, when we learn to dwell in an attitude of

---

[65] John 10.

continual worship, we learn to dwell in the atmosphere of heaven on earth. And thus, the doorway into more of His presence is through thanksgiving and praise.

Praise Ushers Us into His Throne Room

To illustrate this point again, Psalm 108:8 states, "Judah is my scepter." Since Judah means "praise," reworded this could read, 'Praise is God's scepter.' This phrase becomes especially meaningful in the context of the book of Esther, where King Xerxes held out the golden scepter to Esther to invite her into his chamber.[67] Likewise, when God sees the beauty of our praises, He raises His scepter and welcomes us as worshipers into His chamber.[68]

When we praise Him, several things happen. We begin to sense the nearness for which our hearts long and peace settles our souls. As we continue to praise Him from our hearts, we begin to experience joy, and His love surrounds and engulfs us. Praise thwarts the enemy and ushers us into God's presence where all our needs are met spirit, soul, and body.

Praise turns our thoughts from ourselves toward God. Praise is occupied with who God is and what he has done. We praise God when we joyfully acknowledge God's goodness and mercy—when we focus on His character and wondrous acts. Praise and adoration usher us into the holy garden of God's presence.

---

[66] Rev 4:8.

[67] Esther 2:17; 5:2.

[68] Bob Sorge, *Exploring Worship*, (Greenwood, MI: Oasis House, 2001), 6.

We can learn to be increasingly sensitive to His presence so that a simple phrase from our heart of "I love you, Jesus," or "I praise and worship you" brings us into the throne room of His presence where we find peace, love, joy, and rest.

Cultivate God's Presence: A Heart That Worships

Since the Psalms are written songs of praise and worship, use this opportunity to practice connecting with the words and be open to the presence of God's love flowing back to you through the following Psalm.

Exercise Steps:

Step 1. Find a time and place to still and quiet your mind. Focus on the words of Psalm 63 below.

Step 2. Sing or hum the words and try to sense the Spirit of the words. How do these words speak to your heart? Turn the words of the Psalm into a phrase of thanksgiving and praise to the Lord.

Step 3. Do you feel His presence stirring within? Stay in this place of worship as long as possible.

Psalm 63

[1] "O God, You *are* my God;
Early will I seek You;
My soul thirsts for You;
My flesh longs for You
In a dry and thirsty land
Where there is no water.
[2] So I have looked for You in the sanctuary,
To see Your power and Your glory.

³ Because Your lovingkindness *is* better than life,
My lips shall praise You.
⁴ Thus I will bless You while I live;
I will lift up my hands in Your name.
⁵ My soul shall be satisfied as with marrow and fatness,
And my mouth shall praise *You* with joyful lips.

⁶ When I remember You on my bed,
I meditate on You in the *night* watches.
⁷ Because You have been my help,
Therefore in the shadow of Your wings I will rejoice.
⁸ My soul follows close behind You;
Your right hand upholds me.

⁹ But those *who* seek my life, to destroy *it,*
Shall go into the lower parts of the earth.
¹⁰ They shall fall by the sword;
They shall be a portion for jackals.

¹¹ But the king shall rejoice in God;
Everyone who swears by Him shall glory;
But the mouth of those who speak lies shall be stopped."

(Psalm 63 NKJV).

Lifestyle Worship

"Therefore, whether you eat or drink, or whatever you do, do all things for the glory of God" (1 Cor 10:31).

Our praise is a part of worship, yet worship goes further than praise. Praise can be offered to anyone, yet worship is reserved for God alone.

Worship in both the Old and New Testaments is personal and moral fellowship with God. The term "worship" is derived from the word *"worth-ship,"* which is traditionally referred to as the action of human beings in expressing honour to God because He is worthy.[69]

He is the Almighty Creator of the universe, and we are His creation. Satan who was created to worship, fell when he looked to himself instead of God. We humans all have that same tendency to look to our own self-sufficiency. We get caught up in doing our own thing and neglect the One who is our life Source.

This is one reason why worship is so important!

When we live a lifestyle of worship, we live from a sincere heart aware of our sins and God's goodness. We recognize we are the humble creation in need of our Father's loving sustenance. The awareness of our need for God produces a lifestyle of activities lived in honor of our God. We learn to live focused on our intimate ongoing relationship with Him.

Lifestyle worship involves living in ongoing connection with our Lord in everything we do. Our entire life becomes spiritual worship when our heart is continually aware of Him. Then wherever we might be or whatever we may be doing, we are the temple of God's presence—not only for our benefit but also for others. We show forth His glory to those

---

[69] "Worship," D. R. W. Wood, I. H. Marshall, A. R. Millard, J. I. Packer & D. J. Wiseman, eds., *New Bible Dictionary* (3rd ed.) (Leicester, England; Downers Grove, IL: InterVarsity Press, 1996), 1250.

around us by exhibiting His nature of kindness, gentleness, integrity, and love. Whether in work or play, in prayers or activity, all that we do, we do in honor of our Lord.[70]

Special Times of Worship

There are special times of worship where we enter into what my worship-leader-dad calls "high praise." There are times where we enter praise and worship to such a degree that the Holy Spirit enables our worship in union with all of heaven. In these times of worship, our mind may not understand, but our spirit understands. Intellectualism and all that confines is suspended. The Holy Spirit melts all that is wrong and releases pure Love. Years ago, the old timers sang a song that says, "It makes you love everybody." Love is the origin and result of heartfelt worship. The small amount of heartfelt love we express to God is multiplied back in abundance by the Holy Spirit.

This is a deeper level of worship where the true Living Water refreshes the soul. In that moment of glorious rapture, His presence brings peace, love, lightness, strength, and encouragement. God's transforming presence brings special graces to empower, strengthen, and encourage our faith. This kind of worship brings the will of heaven to earth. God's will is done on earth as it is in heaven—for heaven is a culture of worship.

Since we are human, we tend to move in and out of these transforming places, and the enemy of our souls will try his best to distract us. Yet, if we are diligent to find access and attempt to return each time we are drawn away, our inner spirit and soul will grow strong in all areas. When you continually join your heart to the lavish beauty of

---

[70] Col 3:23.

what the Spirit is doing, you begin to notice the transformation in natural things that concern you.

The topic of worship can be large, but briefly, I want to mention that worship is also warfare. When we choose to praise our Creator God, the plans of hell are thwarted, and victory is released. In worship, we breathe our praise to God, and God breathes renewed life into our dry lives. We receive our "second wind." Shame, disappointment, disillusionment, exhaustion, hurt, and fear are all blown away. So, whatever you do, do not lose your praise! This is a weapon available to every born-again royal child of God!

Triumphant Praise

1 Hallelujah! Praise the Lord!
   It's time to sing to God a brand-new song
   so that all his holy people will hear how wonderful he is!
2 May Israel be enthused with joy because of him,
   and may the sons of Zion pour out
   their joyful praises to their King.
3 Break forth with dancing!
   Make music and sing God's praises with the rhythm of drums!
4 For he enjoys his faithful lovers.
   He adorns the humble with his beauty
   and he loves to give them the victory.
5 His godly lovers triumph in the glory of God,
   and their joyful praises will rise even while others sleep.
6 God's high and holy praises fill their mouths,
   for their shouted praises are their weapons of war!
7 These warring weapons will bring vengeance
   on every opposing force and every resistant power—
8 to bind kings with chains and rulers with iron shackles.
9 Praise-filled warriors will enforce

the judgment-doom decreed against their enemies.
This is the glorious honor he gives to all his godly lovers.
Hallelujah! Praise the Lord!
(Psalm 149 TPT).

Cultivate God's Presence: Lifestyle Worship

Worship music is powerful in that it can help us to connect freely with the Spirit of God and thwart the plans of the enemy for our lives. We cannot relegate our spiritual life to an hour and a half on Sunday mornings. Twenty minutes of praise a week does not mean you are living in the Spirit or living a life of worship in His presence.

I urge you to be vigilant to protect your times of praise and worship with your Lord. Do not lose your worship. Satan began to look to himself instead of his God, and his pride arose. His downfall came when he neglected the worship of his Creator.

1. Devote your life to worship in your words and deeds. We worship Him when we put Him first in our daily life.
2. Make a habit to ask God what He wants for your day. You can begin by putting a reminder in your phone's reminder app or the top of your To Do list.
3. A life of worship begins in a heart of gratitude. Gratitude is the heart stance that results in praise and worship. To grow in this area, you can start a gratitude journal or similar exercise that will help you notice the good things each day and give praise. You could make a note of the things you are grateful for each day as a challenge. I have plenty of ideas for this on my website at www.drcynthiajohnson.com/gratitude.

4. Find some new praise & worship music to listen to if it has been a while; make a new playlist. Make a new habit to play worship music sometime during your day (or night). Practice honestly connecting with the words of the praise and be open to the presence of God's love flowing back to you.

5. Decide to notice and work on the words you speak. Eradicate words of negativity and fear. Practice being positive and asking God what He thinks. Put a reminder in your phone. Evaluate the words you have spoken yesterday and today.

6. Share your experiences with someone else you know and/or write about your experiences in your notebook/journal.

Stop and do one of these things right now, before the moment passes!

6 KNOWING THE LIVING WORD

Scripture has depths for an elephant to swim in, and shallows for a lamb to wade. —A saying that dates from Gregory the Great

Ingesting God's Words

"Eat this scroll, and go, speak to the house of Israel." So, I opened my mouth, and He fed me this scroll. He said to me, "Son of man, feed your stomach and fill your body with this scroll which I am giving you."
"Then I ate it, and it was sweet as honey in my mouth. . . Son of man, take into your heart all My words which I will speak to you and listen closely" (Ezek 3:1-10).

IN EZEKIEL 3:10, GOD TOLD EZEKIEL, "Son of man, take into your heart all My words which I will speak to you and listen closely." Ezekiel obeyed God's vision and voice by taking God's words into his heart and life. These are the same important keys He tells each of us today, to take the His words into our inner being and learn to listen closely.

Without the Word in us, we are weak and anemic Christians. Without the Word of God in us we will not be strong enough to overcome the power of the enemy, or even our in-laws, for that matter.

To be honest, when we find time to read the Bible, many of us open it up and do not know where to start. We do not come with the expectation of meeting the Living Word who is ready to speak to our hearts and our needs.

Many times, our view of the Bible is like our view of a reference book stuffed in a drawer somewhere. We bring it out when we have a question or problem, and usually, we use it to justify our own thoughts and opinions.

Sometimes, we come to the Bible with intellect alone. It is common to read the Bible focused only on the words and commands and neglect the Spirit of the Word.

This was also common in Jesus' day. He cautioned those who focused on the words of the law alone. He said, "You search the Scriptures because you think that in them you have eternal life; it is these that testify about Me; and you are unwilling to come to Me so that you may have life" (John 5:39-40).

It is possible to learn confessions of faith, doctrine, and what the Bible teaches about Christ, and become satisfied without experiencing Christ in the words.

Our hearts must yearn to experience the Jesus of the Bible.

As a leader of the Second Great Awakening, Charles Finney wrote,

> Many, understanding the "Confession of Faith" as summarizing the doctrines of the Bible, very much neglect the Bible and rest in a belief of the articles of faith. Others, more cautious and more in earnest, search the Scriptures to see what they say about Christ, but stop short and rest in the formation of correct theological opinions; while others, and they are the only saved class, love the Scriptures intensely because they testify of Jesus.
>
> They search and devour the Scriptures because they tell them who Jesus is and what they may trust Him for. They do not stop short and rest in this testimony; but by an act

of loving trust [they] go directly to Him, to His person, thus joining their souls to Him in a union that receives from Him, by a direct divine communication, the things for which they are led to trust Him.

This is certainly Christian experience. This is receiving from Christ the eternal life which God has given us in Him. This is saving faith. . .

The error to which I call attention does not consist in laying too much stress in teaching and believing the facts and doctrines of the Gospel: but consists in stopping short of trusting the personal Christ for what those facts and doctrines teach us to trust Him, and satisfying ourselves with believing the testimony about Him, instead of committing our souls to Him by an act of loving trust.[71]

One of the enemies' tactics is to try to make the Bible a law rather than the treasured revelation of Jesus Christ. Yet, hungry believers seek the presence of Jesus written in the Bible and receive from Him through the Holy Spirit's illumination things taught in the Bible. Jesus Christ is our Life, and His Words are bread to us. We want to eat God's words like Ezekiel and grow in intimacy with our God.

How to Experience God Through the Bible

"How blessed is the man who does not walk in the counsel of the wicked, Nor stand in the path of sinners, Nor sit in the seat of scoffers!

---

[71] Charles G. Finney, "The Psychology of Faith," *The Independent of New York* (April 30, 1874), (Christian Literature Crusade, Fort Washington, PA) http://www.charlesgfinney.com/1868_75Independent/740430_psych_fa ith.htm.

But his delight is in the law of the Lord, And in His law he meditates day and night.
He will be like a tree firmly planted by streams of water, Which yields its fruit in its season. And its leaf does not wither; And in whatever he does, he prospers." (Psalm 1:1-3).

When I first began to seek God, people told me to read the Bible, and God would speak to me through the Bible. And while their advice is true, I felt like I was missing something. I had read the Bible for many years already, and although I was edified, I longed for more. At that time, I did not know how to recognize God speaking through the Scriptures, and I did not understand what God's presence felt like. My spirit wasn't awake enough to recognize God was with me and trying to make Himself known more intimately. However, I trust that the things I learned along my journey will help you on your journey toward a deeper relationship with God.

The Living Words

The worlds were framed by the word of God.[72] And His speaking creating voice has not been silent through the ages but continues to sound throughout the universe creating and recreating anew.

God spoke to His servants who wrote His words down, and He continues to live in those spoken words. Those words are able to speak to our human hearts today. You see, the Bible is not only a book of knowledge about God but also a living book of God's Words that He illuminates and quickens in our hearts.

However, many people are like I was and do not understand why the Bible is not coming alive to them in a way they long to experience.

What we need is a simple strategy that helps awaken our hearts to hear His words to us personally through those written words in the Bible.

---

[72] Heb 11:3.

We have already discussed in previous sections what His presence feels like and what His voice sounds like. So, now we will examine how an exercise sometimes called Biblical meditation can help us awaken to the Spirit of the words in the Bible.

Biblical meditation can be as simple as thinking about the things of God written in the Bible. We can easily reflect on the things God has done in the Bible, His character and nature, or a verse.

J. I. Packer, the author of the classic book, *Knowing God,* writes that we can turn knowledge about God into the knowledge of God by turning "each truth we learn about God into matter for meditation before God, leading to prayer and praise to God."[73]

In this way, we invite the Holy Spirit Teacher to quicken and bring to life our cognitive knowledge about God. Thus, our cognitive knowledge about God is transformed into revelation and understanding of God and the world around us.

Biblical meditation is a simple exercise we can use to experience the presence and power of our Lord in His written Word. He speaks through the words on the pages of the Bible as we posture ourselves before Him. The Holy Spirit will illuminate the words on the page and speak directly to our hearts to bring life. Jesus said, "It is the Spirit who gives life. . . the words that I have spoken to you are Spirit and are life" (John 6:63).

In these moments of intentional pondering of Scripture, God imparts new energizing life, direction, and edification. He imparts the spirit of wisdom and revelation in the knowledge of God. He longs to open the eyes of our hearts and cause our hearts to burn with passion for Him.[74]

---

[73] J.I. Packer, *Knowing God* (Downers Grove, IL: InterVarsity Press, 1973), 23.

[74] Eph 1:17-18; Luke 24:13-32.

Cultivate God's Presence: Biblical Meditation Exercise

"This Book of the Law shall not depart from your mouth, but **you shall meditate on it day and night***, so that you may be careful to do according to all that is written in it. For then you will make your way prosperous, and then you will have good success." (Joshua 1:8).*

In this exercise, we are going to learn how to experience God through meditating on His living Word, the Bible. Different personalities experience spiritual things in different ways, however, all of us can sense in some degree, even if faint, the signs of God's presence in this exercise.

Expect to sense any of these signs God is moving in your soul. You may sense a feeling of peace, a warmth, or tingling presence. You may have a "knowing." He may give you pictures in your mind. A phrase or word may stand out to you. There may be one word or phrase that stays with you throughout the day. These are all good—they indicate the Living Word is trying to speak to you in some way.

When I first began this exercise, after several mornings, I felt a tingling sensation, not a fear kind of goose-bumpy sensation, but a peaceful goose-bumpy sensation. I didn't understand and didn't know what I was sensing. It took some time for me to understand what I was sensing. And God was sweet to confirm His presence to me in several ways, including by my pastor and mentors.

You should people sense peace and/or joy. God is love and His kingdom is righteousness, peace, and joy in His presence! These are all experiences with the presence of God while meditating on Scripture.

For our exercise here, I have adapted Jeanne Guyon's method of meditating on Scripture, because it offers a deep experience with the Lord and His written Word.[75]

Exercise Steps:

Step 1. Pick a Scripture

The Scripture should interest you and should be simple for this exercise. You can use the suggested Psalm below if you like.

Step 2. Come Quietly and Read

Come to the Lord quietly and read a small portion or phrase. This is not the time to read rapidly from verse to verse. The purpose is to take each phrase in, taste it, and digest what you read.

Step 3. Try to Sense the Words

You may want to take the portion of Scripture that has touched your heart and turn it into a prayer. Only after sensing something of the passage and having extracted a deeper sense of its meaning, then gently move to the next portion.

Do not rush. Take as long as you need. Relax. Take a deep breath. Try to sense and "feel" the meaning. You may ask the Lord how this verse applies to your life. Even if you do not sense an answer, try to sense the Lord's loving presence behind the words on the page. This is our goal for learning to experience His presence.

Then you may want to turn what you sense into a simple prayer from your heart. Here we are not trying to get through Scripture quickly nor say long prayers, but to experience the Lord in the Scripture's words themselves.

---

[75] Guyon, 7-13.

Although Bible study is important, this is not the time for study. You may want to study what you glean later.

The goal of this exercise is to experience the Spirit of wisdom and revelation in His words, then to glean from the Scripture passage what the Lord reveals to you personally.[76]

When the sense of the Lord's presence lifts, move to the next phrase.

Little by little you will come to experience a very rich meditation that flows from your heart directly to the Lord. You will also experience revelations of meaning you have not known or thought about before.

You may spend more time on one verse and none on the others. This is ok. This type of reading is like the bee that penetrates the depths of the flower to remove its deepest nectar.

Step 4. Continue

Continue until you become aware of and sense your Lord's presence. You may want to journal your experience.

Additional Information to Know

You may practice this for minutes, days, or weeks before you experience His presence deeply. Every person is different in the amount of awareness they have cultivated up until this point. This is something that will not work if you are striving. If you have difficulty, relax and find peace. Breathe deeply and let all stress and striving go. Our hearts must be at peace to become aware of His presence.

Receiving from our Lord is like the nursing child who is safe, secure, and at peace lying on its mother's breast. I remember my nursing baby would get so upset sometimes, and I would have to calm her down before she could receive the nourishing life I had for her.

Sometimes we are the same way. We get fretful and worried about so many things. The exercises in this book will help you learn how to come

------

[76] Eph 1:17.

to the Word of Life and be at peace to receive from your Lord abundant life, health, and healing in every area of your life.

It may or may not take many times for you to become aware of God's presence through this exercise. Do not give up. **Repeat this exercise as often as you need to awaken your personal spirit to God's Holy Spirit.** Most of us have spent years developing our minds intellectually, and our spirit has remained weak and oblivious.

This is the very process I practiced many times before I came to a deeper awareness of my Lord's presence. When your spirit awakens to deeper levels of God's presence, all the pursuit will be worth the effort. Our human spirit must learn **how** to be aware of Him and how to respond to His nature.

Now stop and do this exercise before moving on!

Psalm 23: A Psalm of David [with footnotes from NASB]

The Lord is my shepherd, I shall [do] not want.

He makes me lie down in green pastures.

He leads me beside quiet waters [waters of rest].

He restores my soul.

He guides me in the paths of righteousness

For His name's sake.

Even though I walk through the valley of the shadow of death [valley of deep darkness],

I fear no evil [harm], for You are with me;

Your rod and Your staff, they comfort me.

You prepare a table before me in the presence of my enemies;

You have anointed [anoint] my head with oil;

My cup overflows.

[Only] Surely goodness and mercy/lovingkindness will follow me all the days of my life,

And I will [return to] dwell in the house of the Lord forever.

101

7 KNOWING GOD'S PRESENCE IN PRAYER

*Prayer is exhaling the spirit of man and inhaling the spirit of
God. — Edwin Keith*

The Quality of Communication

WHETHER DEVELOPING AN INTIMATE relationship with the
Creator or another human being, developing relationships requires
reciprocal communication and interaction. In the field of psychology
research, the quality of communication and interaction are widely known
to be indicators of relational satisfaction.[77] Humans come to know one
another and develop relationships through communication and
interaction. The quality of communication determines relationship failure
or satisfaction and success.

This continues to hold true when coming into relational intimacy with
our Triune God. Many people cannot speak of satisfaction in their
relationship with God because of a lack of communication and
interaction. To return to the intimate relationship our Creator intended

---

[77] Scott M. Stanley, Howard J. Markman, and Sarah W. Whitton, 2002,
"Communication, Conflict, and Commitment: Insights on the
Foundations of Relationship Success from a National Survey," *Family
Process* 41, no. 4: 659. *Academic Search Complete*, EBSCO*host* (24 April
2012).

from the beginning, we must learn how He communicates and be determined to cultivate a life of spiritual communication in ongoing interactions.

We, as humans, communicate in a wide variety of ways, including talking, writing, thinking, mumbling, shouting, whispering, singing, dancing, art, hand gestures, shrugging, eye rolls, etc.

God also communicates in various ways. For example, He can highlight His written Word, or He can speak directly to our hearts. He can speak through dreams, visions, or pictures. He can call our attention to someone else's words, put a song in our minds, or even put a "knowing" in our hearts.

Jesus says, "My sheep hear My voice, and I know them, and they follow Me" (John 10:27). We must continue to recognize His voice more clearly and distinctly. We can know when He shouts and when He whispers. He calls us to develop our friendship with all kinds of communication and prayers.

The supreme and ultimate purpose of humanity is for intimate fellowship with God. And yet the quality of the relationship is determined by the quality of communication.

There are many types of prayers we can pray from our heart: prayers of thanksgiving, petition, confession, dedication, intercession, and adoration. Prayer is one way we can communicate with God, and it takes many forms and shapes, yet is not intended to be one-sided; it is intended to be reciprocal. God enjoys all kinds of communication with His children.

I want to focus on a specific type of listening prayer in this book, one that overlaps with worship and the experience of Scripture. It is a kind of prayer that focuses on knowing God deeply and intimately.

This type of prayer involves focusing on the Lord and waiting in His presence. It is a sense of continuing fellowship in God's presence. It is a prayer that can be experienced under any conditions, any place, and at any time. It is a prayer that does not come from our mind alone, but from our heart.

We have many examples from our Christian Fathers and Mothers who write about this deep type of prayer experience with God. For example, it is said of Brother Lawrence,

> "That his prayer was nothing else but a sense of the presence of God, his soul being at that time insensible to everything but divine love: and that when the appointed times of prayer were past, he found no difference, because he still continued with God, praising and blessing Him with all his might, so that he passed his life in continual joy."[78]

E.M. Bounds describes this type of prayer:

> The soul which has come into intimate contact with God in the silence of the prayer-chamber is never out of conscious touch with the Father, that the heart is always going out to Him in loving communion, and that the moment the mind is released from the task upon which it is engaged it returns as naturally to God as the bird does to its nest.

---

[78] Brother Lawrence, *The Practice of the Presence of God: Being Conversations and Letters of Nicholas Herman of Lorraine* (Old Tappan, NJ: Spire Books, 1958, 1975), 24.

What a beautiful conception of prayer we get if we regard it in this light, if we view it as a constant fellowship, an unbroken audience with the King. Prayer then loses every vestige of dread which it may once have possessed; we regard it no longer as a duty which must be performed, but rather as a privilege which is to be enjoyed, a rare delight that is always revealing some new beauty.[79]

This type of prayer brings us into the presence of God and teaches us to continue to abide in the vine of His presence. In this next exercise, we will build on previous exercises and practice step-by-step how to experience such a life-changing prayer.

---

[79] E.M. Bounds, *Purpose in Prayer* on Christian Classics Ethereal Library, http://www.ccel.org/ccel/bounds/purpose.html.

Cultivate God's Presence: The Simple Prayer of Presence

How can you learn to pray in this way? Simply start with a Scripture or thought about the Lord, and slowly calm your mind so that you can focus on the Lord's presence. When you come humbly and gently before Him, with a deep sense of love and worship, your awareness of Him increases. It becomes easier to experience His presence more deeply.

This type of prayer may feel awkward at first, but with practice, you will learn how to quickly and easily enter His presence.

Eventually, this prayer can become a continual sense of the Lord's presence that feels like a natural and normal part of everyday life. It becomes as simple as breathing. The next exercise gives specific steps to practice that make this a reality in your life.

Exercise Steps:

Step 1. Find a quiet time and space to practice this exercise. Then come before the Lord humbly, gently, and quietly with a sense of adoration and praise. Acknowledge He is everything and you are nothing. If any sin comes to mind, repent.

Step 2. Start with a thought of thanksgiving and praise to the Lord and come into His presence by faith. If you need help read the following verse very slowly. "Peace I leave with you; my peace I give you" (John 14:27). After you read a phrase, pause, and set your mind on Christ. Express love to Him from your heart. For this exercise, the Scripture is not for study, it is to help quiet your mind and focus on the Lord's presence. In this exercise, we do not focus our intellect, but our spirit to feed upon the Spirit of the Word. We are exercising and developing our spiritual senses.

Step 3. You may want to play some instrumental Christian prayer/soaking music to help your spirit move past your mind's hinderances. In 2 Kings 3:15, Elisha called for the harpist to play, and while the harpist was playing the Lord's presence came upon Elisha.

Stir the coals of love in your heart into a flaming fire by offering Him honest praise from your heart. Stay in this wonderful place of worship and adoration as long as His presence is stirring inside you.

Step 4. When it feels appropriate, gently bring your concerns or request before Him and place it in His hands. Ask any questions you may have, but stay in a place of faith, believing He will provide all things. If the sense of His presence fades, return to loving praise and worship Him. Remain open to His thoughts flowing back to you. You may want to write those down in your notebook/journal.

Even if this type of prayer is awkward at first, continue to practice. With practice, it becomes as easy as breathing. You will experience a deep sweetness of His presence as it ebbs and flows. Stay in the garden of His presence for as long as you can.

Take some time with this method of prayer to learn its subtleties. Continue to come back to these steps for as long as you need them, yes, even weeks and years. This will lead you into a continual sense of the Lord's presence through all life's ups and downs, in quiet times and noisy. For in His presence our human spirit comes in alignment with His Holy Spirit, and in this holy place is everything we need for life and godliness.

Why Can't I Hear God's Voice or Feel God's Presence?

You will seek me and find me when you seek me with all your heart.
Jer 29:13

First, I want to say to you that God is so pleased with you. You are His child created in His image and He loves you! What amazing faith you have for believing in God even when it seems like He is far away. You believe even when you do not see and great is your reward in heaven! We all go through seasons when it seems like God is far away. However, rest assured He is with you and loves you![80] Friend, because you are truly seeking more of Him, you will find more of Him.

Unfortunately, because we live in this fallen world, sometimes it can be difficult to sense our Creator Father in our personal spirits. We spend all our lives training our physical bodies, our minds, and even our emotions. Yet, our personal spirit can remain weak from lack of attention or training.

If you are having a hard time hearing God's voice and sensing God's presence, here are a few tips.

1. You Have Probably Felt God's Presence and Didn't Realize It

For He Himself has said, "I will never leave you nor forsake you."
Hebrews 13:5

---

[80] Psalms 139; John 3:16.

Many people feel closer to God in nature than anywhere else. So, it's possible you may have felt the presence of God as you were caught up in His peaceful presence during a beautiful moment in nature.[81] Also, many people experience God's presence in a time of praise and worship. So, most likely you have experienced God's presence of peace and love in those moments.

When you experience peace and love, you experience God's presence. God is peace. God is love. These kinds of experiences of God can be steppingstones to a deeper awareness and knowledge of God. So, rejoice, God has not left you. He loves you!

2. Unconfessed Sin and Disappointment Hinder God's Presence

We live in a sinful world that clouds our perception and awareness of God. God has been trying to get his children's attention since Adam and Eve. Our Lord wants us to respond to His love, and He wants us to turn our affections toward Him.

However, our hearts have been covered by a mountain of hurt, fears, unforgiveness, and disappointment through the years. These form a wall that causes our inability to perceive His love for us.

He simply wants us to come to Him honestly and wholeheartedly so that He can heal all that prevents our closeness with Him. If you can't sense His presence, it could be because of unconfessed sin.

So, you will want to take care of that first thing!

Your Creator God is holy, with not even a shadow of darkness in Him. His nature cannot come near sinful humanity until we are covered by Jesus' great sacrifice. Simply ask Him to forgive you. Give Him all your guilt, shame, fear, bitterness, unforgiveness, hurt, anger, stress, failure, or any other thing that comes to mind. Ask Him to show you

---

[81] Rom 1:20.

things in your heart that need forgiveness. He is faithful and just to forgive—if you ask!

Some of you are filled with extreme disappointment. Give your disappointment to God. Tell him all about it and give it to Him.

Do that now!

Ask Him to take those things from your soul. You don't need those things in there. Get rid of them!

Now, don't you feel better? You can begin afresh with hope, wonder, and expectation.

Now your ability for a deeper relationship is restored, and you are ready to experience greater depths of His presence and love! Awesome!

3. It Takes Practice Awakening to More

My dental hygienist took a full set of x-rays the other day. Of course, I wasn't familiar with teeth x-rays, so I didn't recognize anything other than the obvious. But when the doctor looked at them, he saw all the subtle differences in the images. His eyes were trained to discern more than the obvious.

Likewise, in cooperation with the Holy Spirit, we can train our spirit to discern spiritual things we have not noticed before. We are created spirit by our Creator Father, so we already have the capacity to discern His presence. We just need to understand spiritually how His kingdom works and practice being more aware. Truly, we can learn to awaken more and more to His voice and presence every day. If I did it, you can too! Practice the exercises in this little book and they will help you notice His sweet stirring love. You can do this! Keep practicing.

4. Train Your Soul to Be Grateful

If we have been complaining, negative, or gossipy, it will be difficult to hear God clearly. The most important first step I have found is to practice being grateful. The good news is you can train your personal spirit to become more aware of beautiful, peaceful, good, and lovely things. God is good, beautiful, peaceful, and lovely!

We are not born grateful. Parents have to teach toddlers to say please and thank you. We must cultivate the habit of gratitude. I once took an entire year to find and document something I was grateful for each day. Practice seeing something good at least once a day to start. You can use a gratitude journal or notebook, or a notes app. Some people take a picture of something they are grateful for each day.

This is a small exercise that reaps great rewards in your spiritual life! God is good, and we need to learn to notice the good every day!

5. Join Other People in the Body of Christ

If you are having trouble sensing God's voice and presence, a good tip is to find other people/churches who believe in the moving of the Holy Spirit, hearing God's voice, and exercising the gifts of the Spirit.

For example, I wanted to learn about prophecy, so I went to a church that specialized in prophecy. I jumped in and soon I was prophesying too. If you need to receive the baptism of the Holy Spirit, find a church or people that will pray with you to receive and exercise this gift.[82] If you want to grow in faith, find others who have grown in faith to help. If you want to grow in experiencing the presence of God, well find a place that emphasizes God's presence.

When you join your glowing ember with other embers, the embers are stirred up into a flaming fire. You will burn hotter and greater than you could on your own. I pray the Lord directs your steps to the right place for you.

---

[82] See https://www.drcynthiajohnson.com/what-is-the-baptism-gift-of-holy-spirit/.

8 THE ABIDING PRESENCE

*"Thus, says the Lord! Stand [take a stand] by the ways and see [perceive] and ask for **the ancient paths,** [hidden long time ago; in antiquity; the eternal pathway] Where the good way is and walk in it; And you will find rest for your souls." (Jeremiah 6:16).*

The Ancient Path

DO YOU REMEMBER ME TALKING earlier about our family cabin in the mountains of Southern Oregon? To get there, you go up a winding mountain road that turns off onto a gravel driveway, which leads down a ravine and to a fork with one side blocked off. The other side opens to a narrow winding path through tall overgrown trees that block most of the sunlight. Before the path turns out of sight, you can see fallen trees that have been pushed to the side and areas where snake grass has crept to the edge. On a tree, a tattered and fading "No Trespassing" sign hangs lopsided by a rusty nail.

Any outsider would immediately back up, turn around, and leave, not knowing the beauty and treasure that lay beyond the secretive path.

Those of us who know the area, know to continue on the path until we reach a vista of beauty. The views of the surrounding mountains are striking. Springs run into in the clearing that refresh the deer, ducks, and turkeys. Lush vegetation and wildflowers adorn the hillsides. The path may be narrow and winding, but it leads to a peaceful and restful retreat!

At the time of the Prophet Jeremiah's writing, God beseeched Israel to discern which path they were on and seek out the ancient path. In the above verse, the term "ancient path" does not refer to the Mosaic law but the most "ancient" of the ancient paths. It refers to the eternal and everlasting path whose way had been overlooked for ages by God's people.

Israel had forsaken their Creator and His ways. They had made a mess of their lives and their nation. The Lord pleaded with His people to stop the vicious cycle of past mistakes and take a good look at His path, an alternative to their path of rebellion, immorality and hardened hearts. God beseeched them to avert the coming consequences of their sin and return to Him. He gave them a way out of their mess if they would follow the ancient path.

For us too, it is imperative we find this ancient of ancient paths, ask for it, search it out, and walk in it. The path He is talking about is the path to the intimate relationship with God originally found in the Garden of Eden, the path of peace, safety, rest, divine purpose, and relationship.

If you are here, dear reader, congratulations! You are seeking that ancient path of His presence. True happiness is found in taking the ancient path that returns our soul to discover the dwelling place of God's presence.

God's Deepest Desire

"In whom you also are being built together into a dwelling of God in the Spirit" (Eph 2:22).

Adam and Eve knew what it was like to live in the glory of God in Eden. They experienced Him so intimately that they knew the breath of His presence. They knew the joy and oneness of His love. It was paradise to dwell continually at home in the presence of God.

God's deepest desire is to dwell with His family—you and me! Throughout Scripture from the Old Testament to the New, we can feel this deep longing of our Creator Father's heart. Over and over, He says, "I will be their God, and they shall be my people;" and "My dwelling place also will be with them; and I will be their God, and they will be My people" (Jer 31:33; 2 Cor 6:16; Ezek 37:27).

God desires to dwell in and among His people. He always has and always will. This is the primary purpose for which we were created—to love our Lord and enjoy the presence of His love.

Moving From Visitation to Habitation

"Behold, I stand at the door and knock; if anyone hears My voice and opens the door, I will come in to him and will dine with him, and he with Me" (Rev 3:20).[83]

After Adam and Eve's sin disaster, our Creator Father would come to visit His family. His Spirit would rest upon receptive ones in the Old Testament. God's presence dwelt in tents and temples made by human hands, yet the desire to dwell closer to His people propelled Him to come to earth in human flesh.

Since then, the New Covenant in Jesus' blood has made a way for us—His family—to dwell with Him once again. He knocks on the door of our hearts to come in, commune with us, and make His habitation with us. He not only wants to visit, but He wants to unpack and set up housekeeping. He does not want a casual relationship. He wants to make His habitation with us. He wants to dine, but also to stay to do the dishes.

---

[83] Also, 1 John 2:24; Rom 8:9, 11.

Once we open the door, the task then becomes learning how to keep the door open with open access and how to clear the debris from this temple that is our hearts.

What Does It Mean to Abide in Christ?

"Abide in Me, and I in you. As the branch cannot bear fruit of itself unless it abides in the vine, so neither can you unless you abide in Me. I am the vine, you are the branches; he who abides in Me and I in him, he bears much fruit, for apart from Me you can do nothing. If anyone does not abide in Me, he is thrown away as a branch and dries up; and they gather them and cast them into the fire, and they are burned. If you abide in Me, and My words abide in you, ask whatever you wish, and it will be done for you. (John 15:4-7").

We tend to stray so easily. Even when we don't intend to stray, the things of life creep in to clutter our souls. The key to a sustained intimacy with God's presence is found in this concept of abiding.

To "abide" is to continually remain **in** Christ. The word "abide" means to remain in a place, especially as one's permanent or habitual residence. To abide means to dwell, to occupy, even when times get tough. To abide is not simply a one-time feeling, but an ongoing relationship.

The Greek verb translated "abide" in these verses is written in the present tense, which means abiding is not a one-and-done event. There is a continuing action, a continual awareness of His indwelling presence.

Abiding in Christ means there is continual communication and ongoing interaction with the Presence of Christ in our hearts. We practice honesty, communication, and fellowship on a daily, hourly, or even a moment-by-moment basis. To abide in Christ is to practice the presence of God and maintain ongoing interactions.

Christ invites us into a lifestyle of habitation with Him, He says, "come to me," "abide in me," "I am the vine." As the sap—the life—comes into the branches from the vine, so also does His very presence flow into our soul as quickly as we turn our minds from day-to-day situations that compete for our attention and focus on Him. As we turn toward Him, His love permeates our personal spirit. We learn how to open our hearts to receive His precious fellowship. This life-giving flow is the living water that flows from His Spirit to our spirit in sweet communion.

All Born Again Believers Can Practice God's Presence

"By this we know that we abide in Him and He in us, because He has given us of His Spirit" (1 John 4:13).

Christian writers have struggled to express this experience of "living and abiding in Christ." You may hear people talk about this experience in different terms such as union with God, mystic union, transforming union, the unitive way, abiding with Christ, oneness with God, communion with God, fellowship with God, intimate fellowship, and practice of God's presence, among other such terms. Many people consider this experience to be the result of Christian maturity.

However, any born-again believer can experience the magnificent presence of the abiding Christ at any time. We can learn to practice the presence of God from the moment we are born again. We are all children of our Creator Father who desires to abide with us. This is the primary purpose for which we were created, to fellowship with our Creator Father in Spirit and Truth!

The difference between the new baby believer and the mature believer is the depth and magnitude of the experience. A new believer may experience the presence of God irregularly. However, with more experience, the new believer can grow quickly to live in a rich daily communion with God.

Because the Triune God indwells believers by his Spirit, Christians can live in continual awareness of His presence. As they continue to grow in awareness, the reality of His indwelling presence is deepened.[84]

Guard the Ancient Path

"We know that we are of God, and that the whole world lies in the power of the evil one. And we know that the Son of God has come and has given us understanding so that we may know Him who is true; and we are IN HIM who is true, in His Son Jesus Christ. This is the true God and eternal life. Little children, guard yourselves from idols" (1 John 5: 19-21).

The true goal of our Christianity is to know Him, to love Him, to enjoy Him, to live in Him, and continue to know Him. This reality of living in union with Christ means we keep this relationship in the center of our lives and guard it with our life.

In Eden, Adam and Eve neglected to discern truth from the lies spewed by the serpent in the Garden. They neglected to guard the path to the garden of God. They neglected to keep their desire fresh, awareness keen, and receptivity alert.

In the above verse, the Apostle John challenges readers to guard against anything in our daily lives which we might lift above this very truth. It is easy to get caught up in disappointment, hurt, pain, lies, false information, alternative ideas, fears, ungodly or unhealthy relationships, or many other distractions that tend to sneak their way to the center of our lives.

---

[84] John 15:4.

We are to cast down arguments and every high thing that exalts itself against the knowledge of God, and bring every thought into captivity to the obedience of Christ.[85] Those idols try to creep into the center of our lives. However, when we continue to abide in Him, we put a fence around the garden of our heart and guard the ancient path to His presence at the center.

---

[85] 2 Cor 10:5.

Cultivate God's Presence: Practice The Presence of God

Exercise Steps:

Step 1. Quiet your soul in the way that is most helpful to you.

Step 2. Come before Him with a thought of thanksgiving and praise. Turn in to notice His sweet loving presence stirring inside. You may want to play some soft instrumental music. As we come humbly and gently before Him in quietness with a deep sense of love and worship, we begin to increase in our awareness of His presence. We begin to sense when He wraps us up in His embrace.

Step 3. Once you have a sense of His presence, stay in that presence until it fades. His presence is like a fire. You can fan the flame of His presence by stirring your spirit up with praise. In your mind offer to Him a phrase of thanksgiving and praise, then notice His presence spring up inside. Stay in this place as long as possible. This is what the Scriptures talk about as being IN Christ. Christ is in you by His Holy Spirit, and you are in Him.

Step 4. Now try to practice His presence more often at different times of the day in different circumstances until you can continually stay in a sense of His peace. (This is a lifetime pursuit, I know!) If this is difficult go back to the other exercises and do them over and over until it becomes as easy as breathing.

9 KNOWING GOD'S PRESENCE IN COMMUNITY

Two Commandments That Work Together

"He will guide us into all truth and will disclose to us the things to come. The Spirit of God makes known to us the things freely given to us by God" (1 Cor 2:12).

IN THE PREVIOUS PAGES, I have given you some spiritual exercises to develop your intimate relationship with God. However, it is important to note that all personal and intimate work on our relationship with God spills over into our relationships with others.

We must keep Jesus' commands in the forefront of our minds, "'You shall love the Lord your God with all your heart, and with all your soul, and with all your mind.' This is the great and foremost commandment. The second is like it, 'You shall love your neighbor as yourself.' On these two commandments depend the whole Law and the Prophets" (Matthew 22:36-40).

These two commandments work in tandem; they each need the other. We never grow to Christian maturity in one without the other. We are part of the entire body of Christ and need one another. These exercises I have presented for your personal growth have no significance if they are not practiced in recognition that our personal spirituality is to be lived and developed with friends and neighbors. Spiritual exercises such as prayer, Bible reading, worship, study, and fasting have personal and corporate dimensions.

The Outward and Inward Disciplines

In his classic book, *The Celebration of Discipline,* Richard Foster divides spiritual disciplines into three categories: (1) the inward disciplines of meditation, prayer, fasting, and study; (2) the outward disciplines of simplicity, solitude, submission, and service; and (3) the corporate disciplines of confession, worship, guidance, and celebration.[86]

Typically, in the body of Christ, Sunday mornings are structured toward the corporate and outward disciplines, and sometimes the personal inner disciplines are neglected. It is possible that we can know God in the corporate and outward disciplines and continue to remain limited in knowing Him in our inner being. Corporate disciplines, without personal disciplines and personal conviction become a façade that covers our deep need for transformation.[87]

However, without corporate community and accountability, private disciplines have an increased possibility to become twisted in an attempt to keep our relationship with God firmly under our control.

Typically, our human nature desires comfort and equilibrium, which is the very thing that hinders our growth in faith. We try to fit discipleship into our personal agenda, with our personal likes, dislikes, wants, and wishes.

When we genuinely seek God, He will break in and upset our religious systems that try to keep Him "safe" and under control. God will disrupt

---

[86] Richard Foster, *The Celebration of Discipline: The Path to Spiritual Growth* (New York, NY: HarperCollins, 1988).

[87] Mulholland, M. Robert, *Invitation to a Journey: A Road Map for Spiritual Formation* (Downers Grove, IL: InterVarsity Press, 1993), 76.

our normal patterns of life to bring greater understanding, obedience, and dependence on Him.

Often God uses other believers, who we may see as a disturbing intrusion, to be agents of grace on our journey. Brothers and sisters in the faith community become God's means of growth, comfort, support, and encouragement.

The community of faith becomes essential in our personal growth with God. A true community of faith is the by-product of losing our self-sins in favor of servanthood for Christ's sake at His direction. The corporate faith community provides the system of structures and support for our continued success on the Christian journey. We come to faith as individuals, but we grow in community with other believers who make up the worldwide sanctuary of God.[88]

---

[88] 1 Cor 3:9-17; Eph 2:21-22.

Cultivate God's Presence: Your Place in the Body of Christ

1. Do you feel a part of the larger body of Christ? Have you experienced any of the things talked about in the above section?
2. How has another person in the body of Christ helped you to grow spiritually?
3. How can you lay aside your personal interests for those of someone else today?
4. Have you noticed or experienced specific gifts, talents, and abilities? What are those? List them in your notebook/journal. You may want to ask your Lord some questions about those at this point.
5. Ask God where He wants you to be and what He wants you to do. Ask Him for your next step.

The Principle of Rest

Sometimes we get very busy in our serving God, so I want to talk a minute about the principle of rest. The principle of rest can be seen from the very beginning of creation. Our Creator Father, in whose image we are made, on the seventh day of creation, "ceased from labor and was *refreshed*" (Exod 31:17). According to Hebrew scholars, the original Hebrew word for "refreshed" can be rendered "he took a breath."[89] God's example, in the beginning, indicates His intention for humanity to stop and "catch their breath," to refresh themselves physically, spiritually, and emotionally.

In the Garden of Eden, our first parents were put into a safe, sacred, and restful place of fellowship in God's peaceful presence. As we talked about earlier, the word translated "placed/put" literally translated means "set to rest" (Gen 2:8,15). Thus, our Creator Father put Adam and Eve in the Garden of His refreshing, restful presence.

The principle of rest is holy, and when we surrender ourselves to God's care, we experience holy rest, peace, and safety. Unrest comes when we as men and women take ourselves, even unwittingly, out of God's care. God's original intention was that we live this ideal life of rest and peace in His presence.

A Day of Rest in the Old Testament

In the Old Testament, after many years in slavery, the children of Israel had forgotten the ancient principle of rest. God rescued them from brutal taskmasters who refused to allow them to rest. So, lest they forget again, God gave Moses the Ten Commandments, which instituted an entire day of rest for body, soul, and spirit.[90]

---

[89] S. R. Driver, "Ex 31:16–17," *Exodus;* quoted in *The NET Bible First Edition Notes* (Biblical Studies Press, 2006), 345.

However, even when the people obeyed the commandments with their outward lives, most of them continued to disbelieve in their hearts. For forty years God was angry with that generation in the wilderness, because they were stubborn, disobedient, and would not believe. They did not understand God's ways, nor did they try. Very few honored Him with their heart. Thus, they did not enter the rest God had available for them to enter.[91]

The nation of Israel missed their opportunity to find God's intended rest. God swore that they would never enter into His rest because, like Eve, they chose to follow their willful ways rather than God's ways.

Kingdom Rest Now

Even though most of the people in Moses' day did not find the rest of God, the principle and promise of God's rest continue to exist as a perpetual covenant for believers today. It is God's provision for our physical, emotional, and spiritual well-being.

God has and will remain faithful to His promises to take care of His people. There is complete rest, not only at the end of our journey, but here on earth right now as well![92]

The Sabbath day of rest was a physical and perpetual covenant reminder of God's principles for life.[93] These same principles of rest were introduced in creation, lived in the Garden of Eden, and then again reiterated in the Ten Commandments. The Sabbath Rest was the sign of God's eternal covenant of care for His people.

However, in our day and age, Jesus, Himself, is to be our Sabbath rest.[94] Jesus leads us to a greater promise of rest than what Moses or Joshua

---

[90] Exod 31:12-18.

[91] Heb 4:6; 3:19.

[92] Rev 14:13.

[93] Exod 31:16-17.

promised. Jesus, as the last Adam, is our rest and peace. He is the life-giving, refreshing spring of living water who lives inside all true believers.[95]

The seventh-day rest that commemorated the end of creation week and Garden rest were types and shadows of the kind of heart-rest we enjoy in an intimate covenant relationship with Jesus Christ. Jesus completed the redemptive work by restoring the original rest that Adam and Eve forfeited in the Garden.

This is a rest of spirit, soul, and body for those who renounce their own works and trust in the finished work of Jesus.[96] The writer of Hebrews states, "For the one who has entered His [Jesus'] rest has himself also rested from his works, as God did from His" (Heb 4:10). I also like The Passion Translation here, "As we enter into God's faith-rest life we cease from our own works, just as God celebrates his finished works and rests in them" (Heb 4:10 TPT).

When we rest from pushing our own way and agenda, we are free to accept God's perfect stress-less agenda. When we rest from our own striving to produce results and please people, we can trust in God's ability to provide supernaturally. The Sabbath is a gift from God to His people.

Jesus said, "Come to me, all you who are weary and burdened, and I will give you rest." Eugene Peterson paraphrases it this way, "Are you tired? Worn out? Burned out on religion? Come to me. Get away with me and you'll recover your life. I'll show you how to take a real rest. Walk with me and work with me—watch how I do it. Learn the unforced rhythms of grace. I won't lay anything heavy or ill-fitting on you. Keep

---

[94] Luke 6:5.

[95] "So it is written: 'The first man Adam became a living being'; the last Adam, a life-giving spirit" (1 Corinthians 15:45, NIV).

[96] Mark 2:27.

company with me and you'll learn to live freely and lightly" (Matthew 11:28-30 MSG).

Abiding in His presence, brings rest. This God kind of rest is not like our idea of rest. We may think of rest as being relaxation or idleness, but God-rest is living in full alignment (unity) with God—body, soul, and spirit. All creation was established to flow in union and oneness with its Creator. Union with God is peace and rest.

The principle of rest doesn't mean being lazy, it does mean doing God's will God's way. The problem for many believers is we have not learned how to access or stay in the place of God's rest or peace. It takes practice to learn how to live freely and lightly in His abiding rest daily. It takes practice to choose rest over striving.

Strive to Obtain Rest

Hebrews Chapter 4 is the only place the Bible encourages believers to strive to obtain. It says, "Therefore, let us fear if, while a promise remains of entering His rest, any one of you may seem to have come short of it. . . Therefore, let us be diligent [strive ESV, labor KJV] to enter that rest so that no one will fall short" (Heb 4:1; 11).

The promise of God's rest is available in and through our relationship with Christ. Additionally, we should "fear" falling short of this promise of rest. We are to be "diligent" and zealously pursue, push on persistently, and make every effort to enter into God's rest. We should be careful not to miss the opportunity.

What does it mean to strive to find rest? How are we to find this kind of rest? It seems the only striving acceptable is to push aside all that hinders and make space for Jesus in our daily lives. We are to be diligent to make sure our relationship with our Lord is our first priority.

The key to living continuously in God's rest is to have ongoing interactions with Him. We take all our cares to Him, depend on Him, and wait expectantly in His presence. During times in His presence, He strengthens and provides all that is necessary for life and godliness.

Through prayer in His presence, we receive strategies and direction for what to do and when. In His presence is peace and joy. In His presence is rest from struggle to force things in our abilities (flesh). In His presence, we take the position of dependence on Him for all our needs. For He always gives the best ideas and strategies!

I don't know about you, but I continually come back to these principles. We are all growing step by step, day by day, from one glorious moment to another!

Cultivate God's Presence: How to Live in Rest and Peace

"For thus the Lord God, the Holy One of Israel, has said, "In repentance and rest you will be saved, in quietness and trust is your strength" (Isaiah 30:15).
"Casting all your cares [all your anxieties, all your worries, and all your concerns, once and for all] on Him, for He cares about you [with deepest affection, and watches over you very carefully]" (1 Peter 5:7 AMP).
"Therefore, repent and return, so that your sins may be wiped away, in order that times of refreshing may come from the presence of the Lord" (Acts 3:19).

To rest is to rely on the Lord God and to turn your cares over to the One who has intended to carry them from the very beginning. We are the ones who try to carry our troubles by ourselves.

As disciples of Christ, we can learn how to dwell in God's peace and rest. Even in the hardest of circumstances, we can find the flowing springs of living water inside. We can find a place of peace and rest in the inner garden of our soul.

It takes practice to connect with the peace of God in peaceful times so that when we get to the hectic times, we can find His peace and rest there as well.

Exercise Steps:

Step 1. What three things are troubling you at this very moment?

Step 2. Come before the Lord humbly and tell Him you give them to Him. Repent for worrying or trying to work things out on your own. Ask for His opinion on the matter and direction for your next step.

Step 3. In this exercise, practice hearing from God through journaling like we learned earlier. Focus on Him and write what comes from your heart at this moment. Notice the peace and rest of His loving presence. Stay in this place as long as possible.

If you take the time to practice this skill every day, soon you will absolutely begin to see more and more peace in your life!

My Prayer for You: Lord, thank you for these special ones who long for Your kind of rest. I release rivers of living water to flow into their lives. I pray they are refreshed with times of refreshing and strengthening by the Holy Spirit. I pray You answer their hearts' desire and may answers come swiftly. I ask you to bring strength, comfort, and peace. In Jesus, name. Amen.

10 GOD'S GRAND SCHEME

"One generation shall praise Your works to another and shall declare Your mighty acts" (Psa 145:4).

God's Purposes Go Beyond Our Lifetime

THERE IS A DIVINE PROCESS to our lives individually, our lives in the corporate body of Christ, and the world at large. God is not random, but specific about His plans. He works in our lives on every level, in every area. He works in communities and every assignment intersects with other people who are also on this path ordained by our Creator God.

God's divine process also involves generations. God's purpose to allow humanity to function as priests and kings in His kingdom extends from generation to generation. He is the God of Abraham, Isaac, and Jacob. God gave Abraham blessings and promises that were not fully realized in his lifetime. Those promises and blessings for Abraham passed down to Isaac, and then Jacob, and so on.

Likewise, the prayers your grandparents prayed continue to work in your life. And the things God begins in your life, He will continue in future generations through your bloodline. There are no time limitations on prayers because God works outside our idea of time. Hallelujah!

When we awaken to God's purposes for our lives, we awaken into a scene that has been going on since the beginning of time and will continue until the consummation of all things. Your part is integral to the continuing process for the completion of God's glorious eternal plan!

131

Everything We Know, God Graciously Reveals

As we continue to journey on this path of knowing God and experiencing His presence, keep in mind that everything we learn about God and His kingdom, He reveals to us by His grace. Before we can think a right thought about God, He has already done a work in our hearts.[97] A humble mindset keeps us teachable. Everything we see, we see as in an old-fashioned, imperfect mirror.

Ancient Corinth was famous for manufacturing mirrors made of beaten and polished metal that required constant polishing, so much so that a sponge with a pounded pumice stone was generally attached. The vision was imperfect at best, clouded with scratches on an unclear surface.

Like this imperfect mirror, the finite human being can only know in part the majestic and infinite God. Everything we know about God is clouded by our finite humanity. In all that God speaks to us or shows us, we only see and know "in part." This becomes important to realize when we try to interpret and understand what He has given. He may give others in the body of Christ different "parts" of the same picture. In all things, He wants us to seek Him for understanding. It is helpful to continually ask, "What else do I need to know?"

> *"For now we see in a mirror dimly, but then face to face; now I know in part, but then I will know fully just as I also have been fully known" (1 Cor 13:12).*

---

[97] John 6:44.

About the Author

Cynthia K. Johnson is an ordained minister, author, former associate pastor, and a former director of a faith-based women's rehabilitation center. She holds a Bachelor of Arts in Education/English, a Master of Divinity, and a Doctor of Church Ministries and Leadership.

She is passionate about equipping people with practical skills for spiritual growth. When not studying, ministering, or writing, she likes to travel and visit family. She has been married to Howard E. Johnson for 30 years and has three grown daughters and six grandchildren.

If you have been blessed in any way, please share your thoughts on Amazon.com by leaving a review. Reviews play a crucial role in helping others discover the book, and your insights can provide valuable information for readers. I truly appreciate your help in sharing the message of God's loving presence with others! Thank you so very much!

Keep Updated on New Books

Stay in the know about upcoming books by signing up for my email list. I send out a new inspirational, devotional email once a month. Thank you for reading, and I trust you were blessed.

Sign up at www.drcynthiajohnson.com.

Made in the USA
Las Vegas, NV
30 April 2024

89346922R00079